BOUNCING BACK

Geoffrey Norman

BOUNCING
BACK

HOW A HEROIC BAND
OF POWs SURVIVED
VIETNAM

Houghton Mifflin Company · Boston 1990

For information about permission to reproduce selections from
this book, write to Permissions, Houghton Mifflin Company,
2 Park Street, Boston, Massachusetts 02108.

Library of Congress Cataloging-in-Publication Data

Norman, Geoffrey.
Bouncing back : how a heroic band of POWS survived Vietnam /
Geoffrey Norman.
p.   cm.
ISBN 0-395-45186-8
1. Vietnamese Conflict, 1961–1975— Prisoners and prisons, North
Vietnamese.   2. Prisoners of war — United States.   3. Prisoners of
war — Vietnam.   I. Title.
DS559.4.N67   1990   90-4585
959.704'37 — dc20   CIP

Printed in the United States of America

FFG 10 9 8 7 6 5 4 3 2 1

For the men of the
FOURTH ALLIED POW AIR WING,
who endured and prevailed.

ACKNOWLEDGMENTS

Many people were generous with their time in recalling experiences that they would certainly have rather left forgotten. Al Stafford, Charlie Plumb, Tom Hall, Mike Burns, and many others were more than patient, and I am in their debt. The virtues of this book belong to them; errors, inelegancies, and oversights are the fault of the author.

One

WHEN HE WOKE before dawn, in his small room in "officers' country" aboard the USS *Oriskany*, Al Stafford was having trouble breathing. He lay in his bunk for a few minutes with his eyes open, telling himself that it was all right, that the apprehension that gripped him like a fist was nothing to worry about, probably just the heat. A shower would make him feel better.

It was hot in the South China Sea, and the overworked machinery on the ship made it hotter. The *Oriskany* was an old carrier, laid down in World War II, and straining now to keep up with the demands of its mission, Operation Rolling Thunder. Round-the-clock bombing of North Vietnam had been under way for two years, off and on, and was reaching some kind of climax here in the summer of 1967. The temperature in most of the spaces below decks never went lower than ninety degrees. Farther below, where the enlisted men slept in bunks that were stacked three and four high, ninety was considered cool. Sooner or later the heat would begin to seem like a presence trapped between the steel bulkheads.

And then there was the fatigue. After a few days on Yankee Station, a man would start to feel the fatigue like a weight that he carried around with him everywhere, making everything he did just that much harder. The fatigue got to everyone, from the captain of the ship, who made do with four hours of sleep or less a night, down to the plane handlers, who would collapse on the flight deck, in the shade provided by the wing of a parked airplane, between strikes. But the fatigue bore down most heavily on the pilots.

The Pentagon had run out elaborate computer models and calculations that established the optimum number of missions an aviator could fly over North Vietnam. It came out to one and a half a day. When he visited the *Oriskany*, Secretary of Defense Robert S. McNamara had been irritated to discover that pilots were routinely flying two and three missions a day. There were too many targets and not enough airplanes, officers explained; combat losses were high and replacements slow to arrive. McNamara did not see it that way and sulked through dinner in the *Oriskany*'s wardroom.

One and a half missions would have been demanding enough. From launch to recovery a mission lasted an hour, perhaps an hour and a half, and even a relatively uneventful strike drained a man physically. Even when it had not been especially hot over the target, a pilot's flight suit would be drenched with sweat when he returned to the ship. But time in the cockpit, in the air, was only part of it. The briefings and debriefings required for each mission often lasted longer than the mission itself. Some of the more senior officers in a squadron served as mission strike leaders, and that required extra hours for planning. Then there were the collateral duties, the paperwork that went with keeping a squadron of planes and men functioning in combat. Pilots on Yankee Station worked eighteen-hour days, and the intensity of those days made it hard to sleep even when there was time. It was not at all uncommon for exhausted pilots to stay up at night, crowded into a small room, drinking an unauthorized whiskey or two to relax. This made what sleep they got that much less restful. But Stafford and the other pilots learned to live with fatigue the same as they learned to live with the heat. It became something they worked through the way an athlete plays through pain. It would last until the *Oriskany* stood down for a few days in the Philippines or Hong Kong. The normal rotation was twenty-five days on the line, in combat, followed by five in port. Then there would be a measure of relief, a respite of sorts. But the weight would not be truly lifted until the end of the cruise, and that was still six months away.

On this morning, however, Stafford felt something else, a cold, sinister sensation coiled inside him like a snake. It was the old feeling that comes to men in combat: the feeling that this would be the day; the feeling that your number was up.

There was no firm, specific reason to account for the feeling. But, then, there was every reason. The air war over North Vietnam had entered its deadliest phase, and American losses were reaching intolerable levels. In the first week of its deployment, the *Oriskany*'s air group had lost ten of its seventy-six planes. The combination of conventional anti-aircraft fire and surface-to-air missiles was becoming more and more effective as political restrictions were eased and American planes attacked targets that were increasingly vital to North Vietnam and closer to the heavily defended cities of Hanoi and Haiphong. There was no reason for any pilot to feel immune, every reason for him to feel that he could get it. Some of the best pilots in the fleet already had.

In that bad first week Stafford had seen it happen to one of the navy's finest.

Herb Hunter was a member of another squadron aboard the *Oriskany* and a former member of the Blue Angels, the navy's precision flight demonstration team. Like all of "the Blues," he was known as a red-hot pilot, a man who could really *fly* that airplane. He flew an F-8, a pure fighter de-signed for air-to-air combat and modified to carry bombs against flak sites in the Vietnam War. Stafford flew an A-4, the navy's primary tactical bomber, the plane that carried the load — and took, by far, most of the losses — in the car-rier war over North Vietnam.

On a day when Hunter led a mission against a railroad bridge twenty-five miles south of Hanoi, Stafford had been assigned to fly the "wet wing tanker," an A-4 that carried external fuel tanks and a hose that could be used for emer-gency midair refueling of any strike planes that returned to the ship low on gas. This was a milk run, the sort of assign-ment a pilot might draw once a month and for which he would be grateful. The worst that could happen would be that he might have to fly over the beach to refuel a damaged plane that would not otherwise make it to the ship, or the water. But more often than not, nothing happened between launch and recovery, and the pilot merely flew wide circles over the Gulf of Tonkin.

While he was orbiting the ships of Task Force 77, listen-ing to the radio transmissions of the striking aircraft, Staf-ford heard Hunter report that he had taken a hit in his wing and was losing fuel. He was headed for the ship but did not know if he could make it at his current loss rate.

Stafford called for a plot and course and took a heading to intercept. A minute or two later he saw Hunter's plane, leaking a long trail of fuel. Stafford got Hunter on the radio and told him he had him visually and was prepared to give him fuel. The planes closed, and when they were still five miles apart, Stafford pulled an Immelmann. The maneuver put him on a course exactly opposite the one he had been flying and which matched Hunter's course at the same alti-tude. Then Stafford popped the fuel hose so Hunter could plug in. It was the sort of flying a Blue Angel ought to ap-preciate, Stafford thought.

But skillful as the maneuver had been, it did not help Hunter, who had lost hydraulics. Stafford had flown F-8s in another squadron, and he realized that without hydraulics, the F-8's fuel probe could not be extended.

"Nice try," Hunter said.

Stafford retracted the fuel hose and took a position above Hunter's plane to inspect the damage. In the left wing he saw a hole the size of a basketball, more than big enough to weaken the wing. Worse, two bombs weighing half a ton still hung on the rack under that wing and would not release when Hunter tried to drop them. Although they would not explode when the plane landed, the extra weight might be too much for the damaged wing.

"Herb, I think you ought to get out of that airplane," Stafford said, describing the damage.

"I can land it," Hunter said.

"I can see blue water through that hole," Stafford said. "You've lost a lot of wing."

"Roger."

"Just get it close to the ship and punch out."

"I'm going to put it on the ship," Hunter said. "Now let me fly this airplane." There had been some concern in the fleet that too many planes that could be salvaged were being abandoned, and this might have accounted for Hunter's determination not to eject. Whatever the reason, it was his call and Stafford had to respect it, one pilot to another.

"Roger," he said and went off the air. Hunter did not need any distractions.

Stafford flew the rest of the way above Hunter, who had decided to try landing on the *Bon Homme Richard*, a carrier thirty miles closer to the beach than the *Oriskany*. Hunter was so low on fuel that he did not even fly the normal pattern — down the starboard side of the ship, then around, into the groove. Instead he flew a straight-in approach. The landing signal officer aboard the *Bon Homme Richard* had been alerted and was ready to help Hunter bring the plane down. The normal tension of carrier flight operations had been raised a level or two by the emergency. There was a sense of urgency in the radio traffic but nothing approaching alarm or panic. Pilots came back shot up all the time, and Herb Hunter was a damned good pilot.

Stafford watched from his escorting position above as Hunter brought the F-8, in its characteristic nose-high landing attitude, into final. Since he had no hydraulics, he had to blow his wheels down into position with emergency air, and he was unable to elevate the F-8's wing into its raised position. He was coming in fast, but it was still a good approach.

Hunter made it over the ramp and took a cut. The plane dropped onto the deck. Then, in less time than would have seemed possible, the damaged wing buckled, throwing the tail of the aircraft up into the air so that the arresting hook glided impotently over the cables stretched across the flight deck. The plane skidded across the deck at one hundred knots and fell over the side. Stafford saw a small puff of smoke from the ignition of the last of Hunter's fuel. When he came back around for another pass, he could make out the ghostly white form of a deployed parachute underwater. The crash had somehow triggered the ejection system of Hunter's plane. His body was recovered by the helicopter that flew plane guard.

That had happened six weeks earlier, just a few days into the cruise, and like the other pilots on Yankee Station, Stafford had put it behind him. He was a professional. That was the foundation of an aviator's pride — his professionalism. Somebody in Washington devised the strategy, more or less, and cleared the targets. Command, in Hawaii, sent out the frag order, and the air group briefed each mission. Then the pilots went out and did the job. Two or three or even four missions a day. But if anyone had ever believed that it was going to be easy or that simply being a good pilot would be enough to guarantee survival, then what had happened to Herb Hunter had quickly disabused him.

As he lay in his bunk trying to control his breathing, to change the shallow gasps into a deep, steady rhythm, Stafford thought about Herb Hunter and the other pilots in the air group who had been shot down, some captured and some killed and some declared missing, their status uncertain. It was dangerous to think about these things but sometimes unavoidable. Even professionalism had its limits.

Stafford told himself that it was normal to feel the way he did. It was a case of nerves and he'd get over it once he was in the cockpit. Every pilot lived with the feeling, he told himself, and even if the men never talked about it, some got up and vomited first thing, then briefed and flew their missions. One of his closest friends in the squadron, a man with a civilian airliner job waiting for him in the States and who had flown enough combat that he was technically entitled to go home, did this every morning.

"Jesus Christ," he would say to Stafford after he'd thrown up his breakfast, "I just don't know how much more of this I can take. I'm a real goddamned basket case."

"You could go home," Stafford would say. "Why don't you?"

"Point of personal honor," the man would say. And then he would go out and fly another mission. And fly it well. The man was one of the better pilots in the squadron. He had helped Stafford through one rough mission, after he'd lost his wingman to a missile.

Stafford got out of the bunk and showered quickly. Wet down, soap down, wash down, according to the formula for a ship at sea, running a constant shortage of fresh water.

The shower did not do much to relieve the heat or Stafford's nerves. He dressed. Under his flight suit he wore a T-shirt with the words "Eat at the East End" stenciled across the chest. The East End was a Subic Bay bar and whorehouse frequented by enlisted men. A shabby, end-of-the-road bucket of blood. One of the pilots in the squadron had made a stencil from a piece of laundry cardboard. Beneath the lettering, in green paint, there was a crude but accurate silhouette map of Vietnam. The pilot had sprayed the stencil on the T-shirts of just about everyone in the squadron. Most of the pilots had thrown theirs away, but Stafford wore his. It was part of his persona, part of his role within the squadron. If it was one pilot's role to stencil the T-shirts, it was Stafford's to be the only pilot in the squadron to wear his. Squadron humor depended on roles, and Stafford played his unfailingly.

Before leaving his room, Stafford zipped his flight suit up high enough to cover the inscription.

After a quick, light breakfast in the wardroom, he made his way to the squadron ready room to be briefed for the day's mission. The shower had not helped and neither had the breakfast. The cold, queasy feeling was still there.

The ready room was designed and located with pilot efficiency in mind. About the size of a living room — forty by twenty feet — it was two levels below the flight deck, a little forward of midships, so that when they left after a briefing, weighted down with G-suits and survival harnesses, the pilots would not have far to go to get to their airplanes. It was also air-conditioned.

The ready room was the focal point of squadron life. Pilots spent more time there than in their rooms or the ship's wardroom, where the nonflying officers relaxed when they were off duty. The ready room held sixteen leather-covered chairs that looked as though they had been salvaged from an old movie theater. They were cracked and stained from the sweat of pilots who sat in them to listen to mission briefings, follow the flight deck action on closed-circuit television, or watch movies at night. Enlarged reconnaissance photographs of targets hung from the bulkheads. Duty rosters, the plan of the day, and the usual official military notices were posted on the bulletin board. There was a coffeepot and a rack of mugs on one bulkhead and a line of G-suits and survival harnesses hanging from another. The ready room was a busy place that had a lot in common with a locker room. It felt, and smelled, the same.

Ordinarily Stafford would take a sort of comfort, a measure of security, from merely being in the ready room with the other pilots from VA-163. They were his comrades, his only true peers. He did not actually know many of the four thousand officers or enlisted men who made up the ship's company. He was assigned to the air group, and the air group happened to be stationed aboard the *Oriskany*. And while he knew pilots in the other squadrons that made up the air group — some of them very well, going all the way back to flight training in Pensacola twelve years earlier — he was not close to them the way he was to the other fifteen pilots in his own squadron, which was the irreducible unit. Stafford's loyalty to the squadron was total.

He had strenuously requested this duty, making a personal appeal to an admiral who had called him in a few months earlier to acknowledge his work on another, non-flying assignment. In stiff, formal fashion the admiral had complimented Stafford for his good work on his recent job in Thailand, telling him that the country's king and queen had mentioned him by name in their correspondence. It was good for a letter in his jacket and a commendation medal.

When the admiral finished this short, pro forma statement of official gratitude, Stafford did something he had lain awake all night planning.

"Thank you, Admiral," he said, "I appreciate it. I enjoyed

the assignment and I'll work hard on the next one. But, sir, there is something I'd like to ask you, if I can have a minute of your time."

The admiral blinked with mild surprise. Junior staff officers did not ask for an audience with the admiral — not this one, anyway. The chief of staff, who was also in the room, glared at Stafford. But the admiral, who was not an aviator, may have decided that they were men to be indulged. For whatever reason, the admiral said impatiently, "What is it?"

Stafford spoke quickly and with conviction, determined to make his minute of the admiral's time pay off.

He had, he explained, gotten off track in his career. He was assigned to a command that sent aviators out to various amphibious units to provide assistance as forward observers for the marines in Vietnam, among other things. That was how he had come to be attached to the admiral's staff. When he left, he would go back to that command and another nonflying job and from there . . . well, there was no way of knowing. But the way his career had been going, it would probably be shore duty.

"Admiral," he said, "I'm an aviator. I have got to get back to the fleet."

"What kind of assignment do you want?" the admiral asked, still cool.

It was 1965, and in his present job Stafford had seen enough of how the war in Vietnam was being fought to know that tactical bombing, not fighter combat, would be the focus of the air war.

"Sir," he said, "I'd like to be assigned to an A-4 squadron out of Lemoore, California."

The admiral cut his eyes in the chief of staff's direction and said simply, "Look into it."

"Thank you, sir," Stafford said, and that ended the meeting. When he returned to his parent command in the Philippines, he found a set of orders assigning him to the Replacement Air Group (RAG) at Lemoore, flying A-4s. From there he would be assigned to a squadron in an air group deploying to Yankee Station.

While it had been hard for Stafford to get where he was today, it would have been absurdly easy for him to get out.

It was a fact that any naval aviator could take himself off flight status at any time. He simply declared himself unfit to fly and, in effect, turned in his wings. No flight surgeon, no admiral, not even the president could overrule him and make him keep flying. He might be retained on active duty, in the most dead-end, rinky-dink, forlorn duty station that the navy could find for him, but he could not be forced to fly an airplane. Every time he climbed into a cockpit, he was a pure volunteer.

It was not uncommon for a man to turn in his wings when he was assigned to the RAG and realized that he would be flying combat missions over Vietnam in a few months. Pilots felt that if you were going to quit, then this was the time to do it. Another man would be assigned in your place, and the system would continue to function smoothly without you. Pilots who had been together in the RAG would go out to the fleet together. But some men turned in their wings after they had been in the RAG for weeks and the time for deployment was getting uncomfortably close — or worse, after they had been assigned to a squadron and were training for deployment to Vietnam. In that case a replacement might not be fully trained or completely integrated into the squadron. Some resentment inevitably followed when a man quit under these circumstances.

A few men — one or two in Stafford's air group — had actually turned in their wings after the group had been deployed and was flying combat missions. These officers said that they could not in conscience fly bombing missions because of their opposition to the war. This was such an extreme step that the other pilots chose simply to believe them. They could not imagine that anyone would do something like that for any less compelling reason — from simple fear, for instance. Everyone was afraid, according to this reasoning, but a man wouldn't do something like *that,* something that cost him the esteem of his fellow pilots, just because he was afraid he might get killed. It *had* to be something bigger than that.

For that matter, most pilots — including Stafford — held no deep convictions one way or the other about the war. That was a component of their professionalism. They just flew the missions and left the big-think to others. Flying the missions was all they had time for, and thinking just got in the way. They would bitch about the rules of engagement, the chicken-shit targets they were assigned to hit when the meaty stuff lay inside the ten-mile restricted zone around Hanoi; and they would complain that as fast as they bombed road junctions and the like, the Vietnamese would repair and rebuild them; and they would suggest that maybe the thing to do would be send a telegram to Ho Chi Minh offering to push a squadron of A-4s over the side of the ship if he would kindly blow up the Thanh Hoa bridge. But they were not opposed to the war or even discouraged, at this point, by the way it was going. In spite of the escalating cost, they assumed they were winning.

The feeling that had been with Stafford all morning might have made him think about his options fractionally and incoherently, the way you might think about some desperate action that you know you would never take. But there was no chance — none at all — that Stafford would turn in his wings. That choice was no choice at all. He sat down in one of the ready room's cracked leather chairs with his lap-board, a pencil, and charts and concentrated on the briefing for the first mission of the day.

It would be an alpha strike, which meant merely that the objective was a fixed target. The alternative was an armed reconnaissance, which sent planes over an area of North Vietnam where enemy activity had been observed, looking for targets of opportunity. Alpha strikes were more danger-ous, since fixed targets were usually defended targets — well defended if they were important and had been hit before. But pilots preferred alpha strikes, which were considered aggressive and determined actions, to an armed "recce," which often resulted in aimless bombing of suspected choke points and troop concentrations. Planes and pilots had been lost to small-arms fire while cratering roads on armed recces — million-dollar airplanes shot down by basic infan-try weapons handled by militiamen. The craters could be repaired by peasants using wheelbarrows and shovels.

The target of this day's alpha strike was a bridge a few miles south of Haiphong. Twenty A-4s would hit it, making this a fairly large strike. Stafford was not assigned to any of the planes actually slated for the strike. He was on standby, which meant he would go up to the flight deck and sit in a fully armed A-4, ready to take the place of any of the as-signed aircraft that developed last-minute mechanical prob-lems. For some reason this did not ease the feeling that had been with him all morning.

He did his best to ignore it and take down the essential information. Route in. Route out. Radio frequencies and call signs. Target description. Expected enemy opposition. Weather. Checkpoints. The usual, with no fanfare.

When the briefing was completed, the pilots flying the mission put on their G-suits and their torso harnesses. They checked their survival gear — side arms, signal radios, knives, and first aid kits. Then they picked up their maps and helmets and left the ready room for the flight deck.

Stafford preflighted his plane quickly and perfunctorily — there was not much chance that he would find anything wrong after it had been gone over by the enlisted crew. The control surfaces all looked good. The bombs were racked in snug clusters of four under each wing, safety wires in place. There were no signs of fuel or fluid leaks.

Thirty knots of wind, coming over the carrier's bow, did nothing to dampen the heat on the flight deck, and it was hotter still in the tight cockpit of the A-4. Stafford could feel himself sweating under his flight suit and helmet. He would have been able to smell himself if the air were not already foul with the scent of burned JP-4, the most specific smell in a jet pilot's life.

He watched as the handlers motioned the first planes toward the bow, coaxing them into place on the catapults and attaching the shuttle forward of the nose gear and the hold-back cable aft. Then the cat officer swung his arm in a tight circle above his head and the first pilot responded by bringing his plane up to full power. Steel deflectors sent the blast straight up into the air above the flight deck, like flames from some incredibly hot furnace. Finally, with the plane quivering against the restraining hold-back cable, the cat officer dropped to one knee and the cat was fired. The plane surged down the deck, clearing it in less than a second, traveling now at 160 knots and straining for altitude above the lead-gray surface of the water. Stafford watched each shot intently. Like all naval aviators he was still fascinated by carrier ops and could watch launches and recoveries for hours.

While he watched, one of the A-4s in front of him moved tentatively toward the catapults and then stopped. The canopy of the ship came back up, and Stafford saw the pilot make a motion with the flat of his hand, drawing it across his throat. For some reason the pilot was scrubbing; there was a malfunction in his airplane and he would not fly the mission.

The plane handlers moved in and pushed the crippled A-4 out of the way. Then one of them pointed at Stafford and motioned for him to bring his A-4 up to the cat for launch. As he eased off the brakes and the plane started hesitantly forward, Stafford glanced at the crippled plane and saw that the pilot was John Roosen. They had flown together in another squadron a few years earlier. They were friends and had closed the officers' club bar together many times. Roosen had come over to the *Oriskany* as a replacement after a fire on the *Forrestal* had killed 132 men. The fire had cooked off some sixteen bombs on the flight deck, and at one point Roosen had led an improvised damage-control party, passing bombs and rockets, bucket-brigade fashion, away from the fire and then jettisoning them over the side of the ship. According to word in the fleet, Roosen had saved numerous lives and risked his own boldly enough to be recommended for a Navy Cross. Whatever the A-4's problem, Stafford thought, it was genuine. Roosen wouldn't fake it to get out of the mission. As the planes passed on the busy flight deck, Roosen looked at Stafford, shook his head, and held up his hands helplessly. Stafford nodded back to show he understood the meaning of Roosen's gesture. It would be twenty years before they saw each other again.

Two

I T WAS a good launch. The little A-4 had to struggle for altitude under its heavy bomb load. But that was routine, and Stafford climbed uneventfully to twelve thousand feet, where he made the planned rendezvous with an orbiting tanker that was assigned to fill the striking planes' tanks, left nearly empty to lighten them for the cat shot. Stafford closed on the tanker and found the basket with his probe on the first try. There was nothing wrong with his flying.

This was the normal experience for a pilot. No matter how tightly the tension seemed to grip him between missions or during a briefing, once he was in the air, flying the airplane and concentrating on business, there was no time to be afraid. Waiting was always harder than flying.

When he'd topped his tanks and disengaged, Stafford joined the other planes flying the mission. They made a loose formation and headed for the target. There was no radio chatter, nor would there be any until they had crossed the coastline of Vietnam and the leader called back to the officers plotting the raid aboard the ship to report that the formation was "feet dry." Radio silence came easy to the pilots. They had done it all before; there was nothing to talk about.

A few minutes before the "feet dry" call, Stafford began

to hear the hum of enemy radar in his headset. It reminded him, vaguely, of the sound of an orchestra tuning up before a concert.

"Feet dry."

The coast of Vietnam showed green and mountainous twelve thousand feet below the formation. In other circumstances Stafford would probably have studied the intricate maze of bays, coves, and inlets beneath his wing. He had been raised on the Eastern Shore of Maryland, near where the Choptank River flows into the Chesapeake Bay. Next to flying, what he loved most was sailing. Wherever the navy sent him, he would find himself wondering just how good the sailing would be compared to the Chesapeake, which he considered the standard for all comparisons. But today, and on every mission over Vietnam, the coastline was simply a landmark. *Feet dry.* Time to clean up the airplane, make sure your bombs were armed, look over the cockpit, close up a little on the leader, and get your mind on business.

Once they were over the beach, the land below spread out in an intricately gridded system of rice paddies, flat and orderly and pale green. The planes climbed. It helped to start your roll in with as much extra altitude as possible. You could exchange altitude for speed when you had to dive to get away from the surface-to-air missiles, the SAMs. Pilots believed that over Vietnam, speed was life.

As the attacking planes closed on the target, there was a new sound in Stafford's headset, a warble from the SAMs' radar, tracking and acquiring targets. Four escorting F-8s, a pair on each flank of the A-4s, went to afterburner and accelerated ahead of the strike planes to engage flak sites that defended the target. The formation was at sixteen thousand feet, twenty seconds from the point where the planes would begin to roll in on the target.

The radio had come alive. The leader of the strike was

the squadron commander, Brian Compton, one of those born combat leaders. When he told the other pilots to close on him and prepare to roll in on the target, they did it without thinking. This was a moment of intense concentration, high tension, and surging adrenalin. The sound of Compton's voice, with his distinct Alabama accent, gave them an extra measure of confidence.

Stafford's SAM warning device began to chatter. This meant a missile had been launched — that much was certain. But there was no way of knowing, without seeing the missile and establishing its relative bearing, whether it was tracking him or another plane in the attacking group. In his rearview mirror Stafford saw his wingman dip across the formation to take a tighter position. This was the last maneuver before roll in, now about five seconds away.

Stafford had to make a decision. He could break off the attack and dive. If a SAM was tracking him, the violence of the maneuver would throw it off course. Or he could follow Compton, continue the attack, and hope that the SAM was tracking another plane or that the range was great enough that he could make the attack and still shake the missile. This last was a remote hope. He was traveling at some five hundred knots, and the missile could reach Mach 2 shortly after launch. At those speeds, five seconds was enough time to eat up a lot of distance.

The cockpit was full of radio chatter and the scolding sound of the missile warning device. The other planes were out there at his wing tips and in front of him. Below was the target and the blooming orange bursts of heavy-caliber guns, seeking the range as the planes began their dives. Everything, as usual, was happening at once — too fast for a man to take it all in. The only solution to this overload was to focus on the target, on the lead plane, and the sturdy sound of Brian Compton's voice. "Let's close it up now and commence roll in."

In the midst of all this, Stafford made his decision, like a man flipping a coin or turning a card. He stayed with the attack. He could never be sure whether that was the instinctive act of a combat aviator or the impulse of a weary man seized by the feeling that his time was up.

He saw one missile soar past him, trailing flame. It looked like a flying telephone pole, the way everyone described it. The second missile, the one that had been tracking him, struck his plane amidships, just behind the cockpit. The three-hundred-pound warhead exploded and cooked off the four tons of bombs under Stafford's wings and belly along with some eight thousand pounds of jet fuel. He and his plane disappeared in a rolling black and orange fireball.

As the rest of the formation pressed the attack, two other planes were shot down by the same barrage of SAMs. One of them belonged to Stafford's wingman, whose engine ingested fragments from Stafford's plane. The engine exploded, blowing the tail off the A-4, and Stafford's wingman went into an inverted spin which he fought for ten thousand feet before he gave up and ejected. The other plane was not severely damaged, but the pilot was seriously wounded. He nursed the plane out over the gulf and ejected. He died in the water before the helicopter could rescue him.

In the confusion none of the other pilots saw exactly what happened to Stafford. None had any reason to think there would be anything to see. They did spot one parachute but assumed, when they discussed it later, that it belonged to Stafford's wingman. They also heard the sound of a pilot's survival radio and assumed that it came from the wingman. With what little time they had to consider it, they concluded that Stafford was dead, blown to pieces by the fireball.

In fact, the armor plating behind his seat had protected Stafford from the concussion of the initial explosion. He was knocked unconscious and tumbled away from the fireball, still attached to his seat. The force of the explosion triggered the automatic sequence that fired the ejection seat in an emergency on the ground, first separating the pilot from his seat and then immediately deploying his parachute, overriding the barometric device that operated when the pilot was at high altitude. So, at about twelve thousand feet over North Vietnam, Stafford regained consciousness at the moment when his parachute opened *below* him. A couple of panels in the chute had been blown away, and he could see the green of the rice paddies through them. Then he fell past the parachute and began to oscillate below it. One leg was tangled in a suspension line and his flight suit was on fire, smoldering like burning bedding.

Stafford's first thought was, *Well, now I know.* Pilots always said you could only finish a cruise in one of three ways — killed, captured, or by going home. Now he knew.

I won't have to get up in the morning and worry about it anymore.

He reached around to slap at the suit where it was burning, but his left arm would not work and he realized that it was broken. He tried the other arm, discovered that it was all right, and put out the fire. But the movement sent a sharp shock of pain through his upper body. It was clear that he had also broken several ribs.

Stafford looked up at the parachute. Through the gaps where the panels had been blown or burned out he could see the dazzling blue sky above him. He strained to reach his foot and free it from the suspension line.

Though still stunned from the explosion, Stafford was suddenly determined not to die hitting the ground head first hanging from a parachute. That would be an insupportable death for a fighter pilot. Too undignified.

He kept struggling to free his foot from the suspension line, despite the pain from his broken ribs. It was not easy with one broken arm, but he managed to work the loop of nylon down over his boot until his foot was released. Then, as he began to go through the procedure to prepare for a parachute landing, he suddenly couldn't see. For a moment he thought he had been blinded. He raised his good hand to his face and brought it away wet with blood. A lot of blood. For a panicky moment Stafford thought he might bleed to death before his parachute hit the ground. Then he told himself that wounds to the head and face always bleed a lot. Probably just Plexiglas from his shattered canopy. No sweat.

He began to do what he could as he drifted down into Vietnam. There was, he knew, no chance of escape or rescue. He was bagged.

He used his survival radio to make one transmission: a call to Compton. "Sorry, boss," Stafford said. "I'll see you after the war." Then he threw the radio away. Word among aviators was that it could be dangerous to be captured holding a radio. Men had been tortured to make them call for a rescue on ground where the North Vietnamese had laid an ambush. There was a story about two air force pilots who had been captured together in Laos. One had been mutilated, virtually skinned alive, to convince the other to call for a rescue on his survival radio.

He also got rid of a signal scarf and a package of morphine Syrettes, even though they would help kill the pain. In a medical briefing he had learned that he carried enough morphine to kill himself and now thought he might actually be tempted. The idea was repellent. He thought about getting rid of the .38 pistol he carried on his survival harness but decided against it.

Slowly, North Vietnam seemed to rise toward him. He tried to steer the chute, but with his arm broken he could not pull down effectively on the risers. He came down in a pigpen or chicken coop — he could not tell which — crashing through the thatched roof and further damaging his ribs, then landing on his bad shoulder in a large puddle of mud.

He lay face down with his weight on his knees, unable to use his bad arm to push his face and chest off the ground. His next thought was that he might drown in a few inches of water, tangled in his parachute. Then he heard the sound of something striking the ground a few inches from his face and an unmistakable crack. He knew that he was being shot at.

He made it out of the mud and found himself facing, not ten feet away, a boy in ragged khakis, who was holding an old French infantry rifle. The weapon had no magazine, and the boy was loading another round into the breech. He closed the bolt, raised the rifle, and fired. The round went past Stafford's head just as he was reaching for his pistol. He cocked the pistol and aimed it at the boy. The boy looked up from trying to reload the rifle and saw Stafford, covered with mud, his face smeared with blood, a pistol in his hand. The boy froze. For a few seconds the two of them remained locked in some kind of private standoff.

Stafford noticed a jeep coming down a road and assumed it was the militia. Then an old wrinkled woman dressed in black pajamas appeared on a rice paddy dike that surrounded the village and served as a trail. She shouted something to Stafford through teeth stained black with betel nut.

He knew no Vietnamese but he understood, somehow, that she was saying, "Don't shoot the boy." He shouted back, in English, "Tell the boy not to shoot the pilot."

She said something to the boy. He lowered the rifle. Stafford said, "Tell him to throw it away." He gestured to indicate what he wanted.

The old woman spoke to the boy again. He threw the rifle to his side. Stafford opened the cylinder of his pistol and shook the rounds out, then threw it aside. At just about that moment, a group of peasants arrived.

They surrounded Stafford, and while some held his arms, others cut his parachute, harness, boots, and flight suit away. When they had stripped him to his shorts and taken his watch, they tried to remove his wedding ring. But it was too tight, so one of the peasants began to saw on Stafford's finger with an old, rusty knife. He had taken one stroke when the old woman stepped in and began talking angrily and shaking her finger at the man with the knife. Stafford quickly worked the ring off his bleeding finger and gave it to one of the peasants.

Stunned and in some form of shock, he stood helplessly, surrounded by shouting and shoving peasants, waiting for whatever might happen next, feeling neither pain nor fear. Everything, including his broken arm, simply felt numb.

A few minutes later a squad of militiamen arrived and took custody of the new American prisoner in a formal, almost ceremonial fashion. They did not scream and push but merely tied Stafford's hands behind his back and motioned for him to march down the dike. Before he left, he searched the crowd for the old woman. When he found her Stafford nodded, and, without expression but in a way that he thought was sympathetic, she nodded back.

He did not know where the militiamen were taking him. It made no difference anyway. He simply walked, awkwardly, feeling the first spasms of pain in his arm and trying not to lose his balance and fall off the narrow dike into the water on either side. The men behind him urged him on with bayonets and words he did not understand, spoken in high-pitched, cacophonous voices that added to the sense of unreality of everything that was happening to him.

They walked like this for what seemed a mile or more. It was difficult to judge distance or time. Walking was not easy.

He could not balance with his hands tied behind him and his arm broken and beginning, now, to throb. He stumbled several times, and when he pulled up, gasping from the pain in his rib cage, the militiamen pushed him and prodded him with bayonets and rifle stocks. Stafford screamed obscenities, which the militiamen ignored.

Then, suddenly and for no apparent reason, they stopped. Stafford was forced to kneel on the edge of the dike. The militiamen checked their rifles to make sure they were loaded. Stafford could hear the sound of metal on metal when the bolts closed. He shut his eyes and for a moment he felt a kind of surpassing calmness.

Well, now I won't have to worry about whether I can take this, or anything else, ever again.

He waited, with his eyes closed and his insides going cold, for something, the sound or the impact of bullets. What he heard was the click of a camera shutter and, when he flinched, laughter. It was a phony execution, a pointless gesture of torment. Stafford felt weak in the legs and his mouth was very dry when they made him stand up and begin walking again.

Eventually the little formation reached the outskirts of Haiphong and what looked like some kind of police substation with a one-cell jail. Stafford was locked in the cell, where he waited, thirsty and in pain, for what might have been another hour before he met his first interrogator. The man wore a clean, pressed uniform and was obviously regular military. He was accompanied by other men, his subordinates, who stood behind him at a respectful distance. Stafford noticed the man's teeth immediately. They were the color of steel.

It was reassuring, the way that anything familiar is reassuring. The uniform and the steel-colored teeth could have come straight from one of the two survival schools Stafford had been through, where a man was prepared for the experience of being taken prisoner and where the men who played the interrogator's role dressed for the part. For the moment he felt that this was a situation he had trained for and that he was ready.

In heavily accented English the interrogator told Stafford to take a seat across from him at a small, flimsy table.

"State your name," he said, almost as though he were reading from a script.

Stafford also knew his lines. Perfectly.

"Stafford, Hugh Allen."

"Your rank?"

"Lieutenant commander, United States Navy."

"Your serial number."

Stafford recited it.

"Your date of birth?"

"23 February 1935."

That was as far as the script read. Stafford waited for the next question, and for the opportunity to do his duty. It was up to him, now, to resist. Unto death, if it came to that. And he believed — genuinely — that he was capable of doing it. His nerves sang with the kind of fear that was familiar to someone who had landed jets on carriers at night. It might be bad, but it was something you had to get through. Do it right and it would be over.

"Now, Stafford," the interrogator said, "tell us the name of your ship."

Stafford repeated his name, rank, service number, and date of birth.

"You must tell us the name of your ship." The man with the steel teeth did not raise his voice. He did not seem to realize that Stafford was resisting.

Stafford was silent. This was part of his training. First, you should repeat the information you are required to give, just so they know you understand the questions, and after that — nothing.

"You must tell us the name of your ship and squadron. You are not a prisoner of war. You are a criminal."

Silence.

"Name of ship and squadron."

"Fuck you and the horse you rode in on." It was the current, meaningless ready room obscenity. Stafford said it impulsively but also to remind himself of his situation and to make the interrogator understand he was dealing with someone who would not break.

The man with the steel-colored teeth ignored it. "What was the name of your ship?"

Silence.

"Name of ship and squadron, Stafford."

So far it was going the way it was supposed to go, and Stafford felt his confidence rising, as though he were in control. When they saw they had a hard case on their hands, he told himself, then they would leave him alone. That was the way they taught it in survival school. This was the time to make his stand. Once they realized, they would leave him alone.

The interrogator seemed bored. He was looking away, as though he would much rather have been doing something else.

"Name of ship?"

Silence.

"You are a war criminal, not a prisoner of war." This was not a mere technical distinction to the Vietnamese. The treatment of prisoners of war was governed by the Geneva Convention, to which the North Vietnamese were a party. They stipulated that POWs were required to give only name, rank, serial number, and date of birth. Also, that they were not to be mistreated, were allowed to receive and send mail, and could be visited by neutral observers such as the International Red Cross to make sure they were receiving humane treatment. War criminals, to the Vietnamese way of thinking, were entitled to none of these protections or privileges. They were subject to the laws of their captors and could be punished for violating any rules the captors sought fit to impose. Torture was not torture, according to this logic. It was punishment.

"If you do not answer questions and cooperate, you will be punished. If you do cooperate and answer questions, you will receive lenient treatment from the Vietnamese people."

Stafford said nothing. The distinction between prisoner of war and war criminal was meaningless to him, and he knew that the name of his ship was absolutely unimportant in any military sense. He could have told them the truth or told them a lie, picked the name of a ship he had served on during another cruise or a ship from history or simply made up a name. But this was a contest of wills, and, less than six hours after he'd been captured, Stafford still believed he could win it.

"You must tell us the name of your ship or be punished."

Silence.

The interrogator nodded and one of the guards standing behind Stafford hit him. The punch caught him by surprise but it did not hurt. He ducked and rolled with the punches that followed. The beating hurt just enough to make Stafford more determined that he would not be broken. It was worse than survival school but tolerable.

I can handle this shit, he thought.

He pushed himself off the dirt floor with his good arm and sat back in the chair. The interrogator asked him again for the name of his ship.

He refused again and took a few more punches. *Just hang in there,* Stafford told himself. He spit a mouthful of blood. *You can outlast them.*

The interrogator asked, once more, for the name of his

ship. Stafford refused, feeling the muscles in his neck straining as he waited to be hit again.

But the guards did not beat him this time. Instead, without a word, they picked him up out of the chair, took him outside, and stuffed him into a bomb shelter designed for one person. It was a simple section of culvert, sunk upright into the ground, with a manhole cover for a roof. There were thousands like it all over North Vietnam, protection from men like Stafford flying planes and dropping bombs. Stafford went into the small, black space upside-down. He was still shouting when the manhole cover cut off all light and sound from the outside.

The pain in his arm and chest and his thirst quickly became minor concerns. Inside the stifling concrete cylinder he was overwhelmed by the sensation of being trapped and buried alive. At first he could not get enough air. Panic surged through him like electricity. He was sure that he would suffocate in this coffin before they raised the iron cover and let him out. He tried to scream and breathe at the same time.

But nobody came, and screaming used up too much air, so Stafford tried to calm down and breathe regularly. The panic eased, and he was able to turn his shoulders so that he was taking most of his weight on the broad part of his back instead of his head. The movement sent shafts of pain from his broken ribs through his body. It was like breathing something sharp, something that sliced at the inside of his lungs. He tried to use his legs and hands to turn himself upright, but there was not enough space.

But he could move a little, so he would take a position and hold it as long as he could, until the pain was too much, and then he would shift slightly and take a new position. When he changed position, there would be a new shaft of pain in his chest and then some relief. Then the pain would begin again, rising steadily until it was unbearable once more and he would move a little.

Soon he lost all sense of balance and equilibrium. He had no idea whether he was right-side up or upside-down or simply spinning. He had experienced vertigo in the cockpit on occasion but this was worse, much worse. Totally and terrifyingly disorienting, like the whirling nightmare of a child.

It went on and on.

Finally, sometime after dark, the manhole cover was taken off the culvert. Air seemed to rush in like water sluicing down a drain. Stafford filled his lungs gratefully and was hyperventilating when the guards pulled him out. He had no idea how long he had been inside the culvert, no idea of time at all.

The same interrogator was waiting for him at the table, and Stafford sat in the same chair. It seemed to rock violently, and he gripped the seat with his good arm to keep from falling onto the floor. The thin electric light blinded his dilated eyes. He blinked and tried to shut out the glare. When he could stand the light and keep his eyes open, he saw on the table in front of him a piece of wreckage from the tail section of his plane. The name of his ship and squadron were stenciled in neat military lettering across the twisted aluminum skin.

VA-163
USS Oriskany

"Now, Stafford," the man with the steel teeth said, in the same distracted voice, "you will tell us the name of your ship."

He had already gone beyond anything survival school could teach or prepare a man to experience. He told himself that the information they wanted was of no military importance. They could get it from the newspapers, but they didn't even need to go to that much trouble. They had it already. There was no point in going back into the hole to protect the security of that information. This was new territory and he was on his own.

He told the man with the steel teeth the name of his ship and asked for a drink of water.

The interrogator ignored him and nodded to the guards, who forced Stafford to stand. They marched him outside, blindfolded him, and loaded him into the bed of a military truck.

It took twelve hours to reach Hanoi, some fifty miles away. There were long waits during air strikes and while pontoon bridges were moved into place where the hard construction bridges had been destroyed. Stafford was given no water during the trip. It had been almost twenty-four hours since he was shot down and he could not think of anything except his thirst.

The truck came to a final stop a little after dawn. Stafford had managed to work his blindfold loose enough so that he could tilt his head back and see under the corner of the cloth. He looked out from beneath the canvas canopy that covered the bed of the truck. They were parked inside some sort of courtyard. He could hear the sound of atonal Oriental music played on a bamboo flute, the soft gongs from someone striking a tocsin, and water running from a cistern. He saw water dippers made from gourds hanging on a rack, like some kind of still life, and a woman walking through the courtyard carrying two buckets balanced on the ends of a pole which she braced on one shoulder.

This is the camp where they do the brainwashing, he thought. *The one where they play with your mind.*

The truck was parked inside the massive wall of Hoa Lo prison, an evil old compound of several buildings constructed by the French to house the prisoners of their defunct colonial regime. It was a place of misery. POWs called

it the Hanoi Hilton. Stafford was led through the courtyard
to a dreary stone building that was the inner circle of this
particular hell, a place the POWs called the Green Knobby
Room. The color was a pale, sickly shade that recalled pea
soup or bile, and the walls were covered with rough acoustic
tile designed to baffle the sound of screams. The tile was
broken, in spots, from the impact of bodies hitting the walls.

Stafford was seated on a stool, with his hands tied behind
his back. An interrogator entered the room carrying the T-
shirt with the crude stenciling.

"Why do you have a map of Vietnam on your shirt? What
is the significance of 'Eat at the East End'? Is this an escape
code?"

He had already talked, Stafford thought. It couldn't hurt
to talk again, not about something so trivial and silly.

"It's a joke. It doesn't mean anything."

They asked him, again, why he had a map of Vietnam
stenciled on his T-shirt. When he answered again, trying to
sound convincing, one of the guards knocked him off the
stool. He picked himself up and tried to explain again.

He was beaten and kicked and pushed into the wall. His
arm and ribs seemed to burn with pain, but he felt he could
last. The worst was the frustration of trying to make them
believe the truth about the stupid T-shirt.

Finally, after an hour or so, they left, and for a few moments Stafford felt a surge of hope, something close to elation. *That's it. I've done it. I've won. I didn't give them anything
they didn't obviously have, and now they're through with me.* For a
while he was even able to ignore the pain in his arms and
chest.

He was left sitting on the stool with his hands tied behind
his back, and told to remain there. After a few hours he was
able to free his hands, then retie them in front of his body.
Before he did that, he reached over his bad shoulder (he

had also broken his collar bone) to get at something that had been irritating him, an itch like the worst kind of insect bite. When he brought his hand away, he was holding a three-inch piece of shrapnel, a shard, probably, from the casing of the SAM warhead.

He fell off the stool. A guard came into the room and told him he must sit on the stool. The guard noticed that Stafford's hands were tied in front. He paused over this, then shrugged and left them that way.

As time passed, Stafford's awareness shifted away from his physical pain and the uncertainty of his situation and focused on a single fact and sensation: he was thirsty. He was into his second day without water. He had asked for water, in English and French, when he was being beaten to reveal the secret code behind the stenciled T-shirt. The interrogators had ignored him.

He could not think of anything except water. He got down off the stool, onto his knees, and licked the floor where the tiles joined, hoping that some water had accumulated there. When that failed, he tried licking damaged places on the wall, hoping that some water had sweated through.

Stafford spent three days in the Green Knobby Room, without water. He'd had no water on the day that he was shot down, so it had been a total of four days. In survival school he'd been taught that you could go seven days before you died of thirst. Another three days . . . that was impossible. Too much to bear. He was conscious only of his thirst. He was ready to do anything for a drink, and if he could not have water, then he would die and that would put an end to the thirst. He was nothing but the thirst, and dying would end it.

Finally the door to the Green Knobby Room opened and three interrogators stepped in. They had no water.

This time there were no preliminaries. Nothing was said

about name, rank, service number, or date of birth. Nothing about the name of Stafford's ship or the type of airplane he flew. The interrogator began by telling him to name the target he was bombing on the day he was shot down, his air group's next targets, and the bombing tactics to be used in the attack.

To his complete, helpless frustration, he could not remember the name of the target he'd been rolling in on when the SAM hit. It was a set of coordinates and some pictures.

"What is your next target?"

He honestly did not know.

"What is your bombing altitude?"

It all depended.

"What is your wingman's position?"

There was no good answer to that question. The truth was that his wingman flew where the situation called for him to fly. Even if Stafford told the truth, they wouldn't like his answers.

Several guards arrived, carrying ropes and straps, some of them stained with blood. Beginning at the shoulder, they wrapped Stafford's arms, carefully and patiently, tightening each loop until the rope would not take any more tension, then throwing another loop, lower, and then repeating the process, until Stafford's arms were circled with loops of rope like ceremonial bracelets.

When he thought that the pain was as bad as it could be, the guards forced his arms together, behind him, until the elbows were touching, then tied them together. Then his arms were raised toward his head and pulled by a long rope down toward his ankles, which were lashed together. He was being bent into a tight circle.

He was passing out, now, then coming to and blacking out again. Without actually deciding to, he started answering their questions, whether he knew the answer or not, whether there was an answer or not. He began to invent lies and to talk about strikes that were planned against roads and bridges he had already bombed. He talked about people he had flown with years before; made up formations and methods of attack, trying desperately to make them sound convincing. At one point he said, confidently, that his wingman always flew $47\frac{1}{2}$ degrees off to starboard, stepped up $1\frac{1}{2}$ feet. It was meaningless — a wingman flew where he had to fly — but they listened and wrote it down and did not stop him. They had taken the ropes off when he began answering their questions, and as long as he talked, they probably would not tie him up and bend him again. But it was the thirst that had reduced him to this point. He was willing, he realized, to do anything at all for a drink of water. He had lost all resistance, lost all sense of his own humanity. He was an insect, or a rat, crawling around on the filthy floor of the Hanoi Hilton.

Finally his interrogator seemed satisfied with his answers. "You have a good attitude, Stafford," one of the interrogators said. He gave him a small cup of water. Stafford drank it with pitiful, infantile gratitude.

He was taken out of the Green Knobby Room, down a corridor, and out into a courtyard to a bathing area. When he reached the large, full cistern he began drinking from it, gulping the water as fast as he could get it down. The guard pushed him away. The water was for bathing, he pantomimed. Not good to drink. Stafford could not fathom the idea of water that was not good to drink. He would learn later why the water was not for drinking.

He bathed, was given some clean clothes — rough pajamas with alternating red and gray stripes, tops and bottoms, and a pair of Ho Chi Minh sandals made from old truck tires and canvas webbing. Also a toothbrush, a tin cup, a bar of soap, a clay pot for holding drinking water, and a towel. Then he was sent to the prison medical officer, who slapped a cast on his arm without setting it. As he applied the plaster of Paris, the man said, over and over, "Doctor fix."

Stafford was walked down a corridor and into a cell about eight feet deep and four feet wide. There was a window at one end and a concrete slab jutting out from one wall. There were shackles at either end of the slab. A guard brought him something to eat — fish heads and rice. He hadn't believed, until then, that people actually ate such things. He devoured every scrap and decided that it wasn't so bad. He did not know that these were special rations since it was a feast day in Vietnam and that he would crave a meal like this, almost constantly, for the next five years.

When Stafford used the bucket in his cell the first time, his urine was dark brown. He assumed he was passing blood, that his kidneys had been damaged. Actually the color was caused by concentrated iodine resulting from lack of water. His arm and ribs still hurt.

But pain was not the worst, most oppressive element of his condition. That was bearable. The shame was worse. He had been broken; in a few days he had been changed from a man who believed he could resist to the death to a man who would tell his captors whatever they wanted to know for a drink of water. It was the deepest form of depression that he had ever known. Worse than when his parents had divorced. Worse than when he had been divorced himself, won custody of his children, and then lost it, one year later, on appeal. At the time that had been the most devastating thing he could imagine. But this was worse. He had betrayed himself and his comrades. He had sworn himself to standards — to the Code of Conduct — and then not been able to live up to them.

Mingled with the depression there was fear, which only

increased the depression, which then increased the fear. What if they wanted to know more? Would they torture him again? And if they did, then surely he would break even sooner this time. And if he had given them nonessential, harmless stuff before, what was to keep him from giving them something important the next time? He became obsessed by this fear — that he might give them something important; that something more vital than his own honor would be compromised.

The only way to be certain that he would not break, he decided, was to kill himself. So using the few bits of clothing he'd been given — prison pajamas — and some of the gauze from his cast, Stafford fashioned a noose, which he hung from the bars in the window of his cell. Then he stood on the concrete bunk and kicked. The force of the noose coming taut broke up some of the crumbling mortar that anchored the bars around the window. Stafford fell a foot and a half to the floor. He sat there in a heap, with plaster dust floating down on his head, incapable of anything, not even thinking.

The noise from his fall alerted the guards. They picked Stafford up and abruptly broke his cast at the elbow in order to tie his hands behind his back before leading him, once more, to the Green Knobby Room. He was put back in the ropes and questioned, again, about escape attempts and the East End T-shirt. He did not attempt to resist. Again he told them, almost pleading now, that there was no escape plan, that he had not been attempting to escape, that the T-shirt was a joke. "I was trying to kill myself," he said, helplessly, trying to make them believe.

The interrogators seemed to understand that they were dealing with a broken man, that Stafford was telling the truth. But, they said, he would still be punished for damaging his cell and rejecting the lenient treatment and the hospitality of the Vietnamese people. He was untied and sent back to his cell, where the guards tied a rope to his bad arm. The other end of the rope was tied to the undamaged bars in the window of the cell. Then the guards left and locked the door.

A kind of omnipresent pain ran through Stafford's body. Compounding the pain was a feeling that he had been reduced to a kind of insignificance that he hadn't thought possible. He was reminded, for some absurd reason, of his grandfather, who had raised chickens on his farm. Whenever one of his dogs killed a chicken, the old man would tie the chicken carcass around the dog's neck and leave it there until it began to rot and fell off. That dog would never kill a chicken again.

The guards cut Stafford down after six hours or so, then, once again, left him alone in his cell. Stafford spent the next month in solitary with nothing to do, nothing to read, no one to talk to. He knew that there were other Americans inside the prison, but he did not know how to communicate with them.

The days were unrelievedly empty. A gong woke everyone in the morning. An hour or two later a guard brought the first of two meals, usually a bowl of thin pumpkin soup. After that, nothing happened for several hours, until the guard brought another bowl of soup. He would be told, once a day, to put his bucket outside his cell. It was collected and dumped by another prisoner, then returned. Stafford tried, unsuccessfully, to catch a glimpse of the man who gathered and returned the buckets. He looked in his bucket when it was returned, hoping to find a message. There was none.

Stafford left his cell once a week, under guard, to bathe in tepid water in a dim room lined with moldy tile. This took less than a quarter of an hour. Then he would be marched back to his bare cell, with its bucket and concrete bunk, rice mat, and mosquito net. Except for the occasional gecko lizard, he was utterly alone.

Three

MORE THAN two hundred American aviators had been shot down and captured by the North Vietnamese before Al Stafford's A-4 was blown up by a SAM. The first, Lt. (j.g.) Everett Alvarez, had been shot down more than three years earlier in raids ordered by President Lyndon Johnson following the Gulf of Tonkin incident.

For a while the North Vietnamese had treated Alvarez with more curiosity than brutality. The air war had not yet become a full-time, round-the-clock offensive. In fact, there were no raids for months following those in which Alvarez had flown. The United States was engaged in a presidential campaign, and both sides held back, hoping that their caution would influence the election.

During this time Alvarez, the lone POW, was fed well enough, allowed to leave his cell for exercise, and even given some reading material. He was indoctrinated, in a half hearted fashion, with emphasis on Vietnam's history of wars against its various oppressors. More than anything else, he suffered from loneliness and uncertainty.

Like all aviators, Alvarez had been trained to expect something different. In survival school he had been taught first to evade capture if he did find himself on the ground in enemy territory, and then to resist and survive if he was taken prisoner. Survival training was the military's response to the Korean War experience. American POWs had done badly there. Many were enlisted men, not very highly motivated to begin with, and easily manipulated, *brainwashed,* by their captors.

Of the approximately ten thousand men held captive in Korea, an estimated 70 percent collaborated to some degree with the enemy — for example, signing confessions that they had conducted germ warfare and taking part in other propaganda stunts. There were no escapes, and more than a third of the men died in captivity. Morale became an individual concern as military discipline and organization collapsed. Worst of all, sick and wounded men were sometimes left to die untended and were even preyed on by healthy POWs who stole their food, clothing, and medical supplies.

This experience motivated the services to organize programs to prepare their men for captivity in the next war. Survival schools provided hands-on training. Doctrine was formulated in what the services called the Code of Conduct. All servicemen and servicewomen learned the code in the classroom, and its lessons were reenforced on posters displayed on bulletin boards and office walls and on wallet cards that military personnel were required to carry at all times. The code was broken down into six paragraphs:

1. I am an American fighting man. I serve in the forces which guard my country and our way of life. I am prepared to give my life in their defense.
2. I will never surrender of my own free will. If in command I will never surrender my men while they still have the means to resist.
3. If I am captured I will continue to resist by all means available. I will make every effort to escape and aid others to escape. I will accept neither parole nor special favors from the enemy.
4. If I become a prisoner of war, I will keep faith with my

fellow prisoners. I will give no information nor take part in any action which might be harmful to my comrades. If I am senior, I will take command. If not, I will obey the lawful orders of those appointed over me and will back them up in every way.

5. When questioned, should I become a prisoner of war, I am bound to give only name, rank, service number, and date of birth. I will evade answering further questions to the utmost of my ability. I will make no oral or written statements disloyal to my country and its allies or harmful to their cause.

6. I will never forget that I am an American fighting man, responsible for my actions, and dedicated to the principles which made my country free. I will trust in my God and in the United States of America.

Aviators were also taught the code in survival school and given moderately realistic training designed to help them resist harsh treatment. Military men playing the role of guards were allowed to strike prisoners with open, gloved hands. Prisoners were placed in steel lockers for as long as an hour or two. Guards would sometimes beat on the sides of the lockers with sticks. Some men were wired up to old hand-cranked telephones and given electrical shocks to make them sign confessions or collaborate in some other fashion. Training was made as realistic as seemed prudent, given that these were the most highly trained, expensive personnel in all the services.

Along with the physical training, survival school preached a consistent hard line. If you were tough in the beginning, you might be hurt, but things would be easier in the long run. Your captors would leave you alone and concentrate on those who were weak. Toughness was the best defense, and there was no excuse for breaking.

"If they tell you to sign a confession or they'll flatten your balls," the instructors would say, "then if you sign that confession . . . well, you'd better damn sure come home with a pair of flat balls."

Of course, nobody was supposed to be tortured after capture. The Geneva Convention prohibited mistreatment of prisoners of war. Both the United States and North Vietnam had signed. But such protocols tend to break down under the strains of combat. When the bombing escalated again in 1965 after Johnson was reelected and the Vietcong attacked an American base at Pleiku in South Vietnam, more pilots were shot down, and they were not treated as well as Alvarez had been. Nor was he, for that matter.

The North Vietnamese claimed that prisoners were being given "lenient and humane treatment." The Hanoi government maintained, however, that the pilots were not soldiers in a lawful war and were therefore "war criminals." Thus they were not covered by the terms of the Geneva Convention and were subject to arrest, trial, and punishment. It was a distinction the North Vietnamese considered important, and they insisted on it.

The men who were captured after Alvarez were often beaten by the peasants who captured them and pressured in Hanoi until they broke. Then they were put in isolation, often manacled to their bunks. They were fed badly and given little or no medical care. None of this was known to the world at large. The North Vietnamese insisted that the prisoners were still being treated well. Sympathetic journalists were brought in for briefings, tours, and interviews, after which they backed up the claims of the Vietnamese. Some of these visitors claimed that the captured American fliers were being treated better than the Geneva Convention required, better than they had any right to expect.

Treatment, in fact, seemed to vary according to the ferocity of the war. When only Alvarez was being held, no one could say for certain that a state of war actually existed between the United States and North Vietnam. A year later, when there was no longer any doubt, many of the new prisoners in Hoa Lo were kept manacled to their bunks and left to lie in their own filth. When the United States announced a bombing halt, the pressure on the POWs eased just a little. Food got better, and the kinds of small violations of rules that would usually have landed a man in the ropes were ignored or only lightly punished. Then, when the bombing halt ended and areas close to Hanoi that had previously been sanctuaries were bombed, the North Vietnamese bore down harder than before.

The POWs learned several things quickly and emphatically. First, in their situation the Code of Conduct was unrealistic and insufficient. You could resist for a while, but sooner or later you would be broken. After you had resisted "to the utmost of your ability," what did you do? And what sort of statements were harmful to your fellow prisoners and your country's cause? Arguably anything you gave the enemy that he subsequently used for propaganda was harmful to your country's interests. But what about some of the absurd confessions, ludicrously phrased so that anyone would understand that they were not serious and were probably extracted under duress? Somebody, somewhere, might believe such statements to be genuine, so in some ruthlessly abstract sense that confession could be seen as harmful to the nation's cause.

But the distinction didn't matter because, sooner or later, you would break and give them some part or version of what they wanted. And what then?

This was a question that the POWs had to answer for themselves. Over the months and years they developed a new doctrine to fill the gaps where the Code of Conduct and the lessons they had learned at survival school simply did not apply.

It might have been easier, in some ways, if the interrogations and the torture had served a direct military objective. There were some very senior aviators shot down over North

Vietnam, men with experience, training, and knowledge in all sorts of technical and highly classified fields such as electronic countermeasures, nuclear tactics, and antisubmarine warfare. They carried in their heads information that would have been useful to the Soviet Union, allies of the North Vietnamese, if not to the Vietnamese themselves. And, of course, some men did know what targets were likely to be attacked soon, by what means, and with what weapons. Presumably that information would have been valuable — exceedingly so — if it had been extracted quickly.

But the value of all military information degrades with time. The situation changes, and what was critical intelligence yesterday is useless today. The North Vietnamese rarely tried with any urgency to extract this kind of fundamental military information from the men they shot down. When they did go after information about tactics, for instance, it seemed that their actual goal was not to gather data that they could use in combat but to force the man under interrogation to tell them something — even if it was implausible — against his will. The interrogators and torturers worked harder to gain prisoner biographies, confessions, and public apologies than they did to discover anything of real and immediate military value to themselves or their allies.

The point of the torture and brutality and endless interrogations, then, was not to break the men so they would reveal information of military importance. Breaking them *was* the purpose. Propaganda extracted from the sessions in the Green Knobby Room was an almost ritualistic byproduct.

In some eerie, absurd sense, the pilots and their jailers remained at war. In this particular war the Americans were for once at an absolute material disadvantage. While the real war was intensively reported and broadcast, this one was unknown and invisible, conducted in gloom and shadow. It was a war without lines or fronts or any of the other convenient abstractions, and it was fought according to opaque, changing rules. Oriental "face" and Occidental faith were the ruling moral factors. Defeats and victories were simultaneously real and ephemeral, unimaginably important and exceedingly short-lived.

Virtually all the Americans held prisoner in North Vietnam were aviators. A few soldiers captured in the South eventually made their way north, but only a handful. Essentially the POWs were officer pilots, and a pilot shot down over North Vietnam experienced, in addition to physical injuries, an overwhelming psychological and emotional shock. One moment he was the supreme twentieth-century warrior, a modern knight at the controls of one of the most expensive, sophisticated, destructive weapons ever known. And then, in less time than it took to read a newspaper, all of that power was gone, and he was reduced to a helpless parody of the warrior he had been. His armor — flight suit and helmet — was taken from him, along with his clothes. He was stripped to his underwear and tied up by peasants armed with pitchforks and rusty machetes. Pilots accustomed to sleeping in beds with clean sheets, eating hot food off good china, and having their laundry done for them by enlisted men were suddenly reduced to living in conditions that an infantryman would have found harsh and that were for them unimaginable. They used buckets for toilets and had no privacy even for that. They shared space with rats and all manner of insects. And, most degrading of all, when the enemy guards entered their cells, they were forced to stand and bow.

A captured pilot quickly found himself without the security that came from training, routine, and doctrine. Pilots were military professionals who, in spite of a carefully cultivated image of extreme individuality, relied on the book. For every situation in the air there was an approved official solution, learned in years of training. Pilots were resourceful and innovative, but they also believed in going by the book. In captivity the book — the Code of Conduct — was not enough.

Finally, the captured aviator was alone. This was the most terrifying element of his radically new status. An aviator was a military man, and he depended on the service in the abstract, and the group in particular, for his strength. He was an officer in the air force, navy, or marines and a member of his squadron and wing. His sense of professionalism and of belonging to this group, especially the squadron, gave him his emotional bearings and the strength it took to fly his missions day after day.

Like most fighter pilots, Al Stafford was a blend of individualist and team player. A man could not fly single-seat airplanes in combat without believing he was the best. His ego was as important in a way as his eyesight and his reflexes. Fighter pilots were confident, cocky, and supremely proud of their skills. But pilots operated at the end of a long and elaborate chain of support. A carrier pilot like Stafford was one of seventy-six men on a ship with a crew of some four thousand. The mission of every member of that crew was, ultimately, to keep the seventy-six pilots flying. The carrier was escorted by other warships and supplied by oilers and cargo ships. A base in the Philippines existed to keep the ships resupplied and operational. All of that for six dozen men like Stafford. A man did not need a hungry ego to feel elite, important, and, in an odd but logical way, invulnerable. To be suddenly, almost instantly, deprived of all that status was psychologically incapacitating.

Stafford had loved flying and being a part of the squadron in almost equal measure. In his barren cell in Hoa Lo he was separated from both and forced back on his own resources, which were at first meager. Like most pilots he had no gift for introspection; he was not a cerebral man. He had dropped out of St. John's in Annapolis after two years and joined the navy's aviation cadet program, where flying quickly became the point of his life. He lived the pilot's life to the limit, driving a Jaguar XK-140 and drinking stingers at the officers' club, where he told stories while his hands, which he used as airplanes, cut through the clouds of cigar smoke. He had left the navy briefly but discovered that he acutely missed the flying, so he went back on active duty. His first marriage had ended in divorce, and that gave him even more reason to think of himself in terms of what he did — not as a husband or father but as a pilot. He had married again, a few weeks before this cruise, but that did not change the fact that he considered himself, above all, a working aviator.

There was no way Stafford could have been prepared for the loneliness and despair he felt as he sat in his cell in Hanoi. His morale deteriorated by the hour, just as his body had deteriorated from the meager diet and the side effects of torture and untreated wounds. Sitting alone, he would suddenly become aware that he was talking to himself or to the gecko lizard inching along the wall of his cell. Then he would be overcome with the certain sense that he would either die or go insane long before the war ever ended.

Stafford passed that month alone falling deeper into a void of self-pity. Then, late one night, the guards came for him. When the keys turned in the lock to his door, his first thought was that they had come to take him to the Green Knobby Room and put him back in the ropes. His insides turned cold and watery and his legs went weak as he walked out into the dank prison corridor lined with the doors of other cells.

The guards did not take him to the Green Knobby Room but rather outside, to a waiting truck and a guard who held blindfolds and ropes. This guard studied Stafford and looked puzzled. The blindfold would be easy enough, but Stafford was still wearing a cast on his broken arm. It would be impossible to tie his hands behind his back.

Stafford understood the guard's dilemma. Orders were that any prisoner being transported must have his hands tied, and orders were orders. The guard shrugged and broke the cast. Then he tied Stafford's hands behind his back according to regulations. Stafford's arm had not healed, and the pain went through him like a spike.

He lay in the bed of the truck, blindfolded and in agony, as the driver ran through the gears on his way out of the courtyard of Hoa Lo and into the streets of Hanoi. Through his pain Stafford realized that he was not alone in the truck. He did not try to talk to the man, or men, riding with him. The drive lasted an hour or so, and when the truck pulled to a stop, the guards lifted Stafford to the ground.

He could see a little by looking under the corner of his blindfold, but in the weak light it was impossible to distinguish much more than some very large old trees, which surrounded a cluster of low, indistinct structures, and a larger, almost stately building. He was led along a gravel path to a shed with several doors. His sandals made a soft crunching sound on the gravel, and the night air felt wonderfully clean after his foul, unventilated cell at Hoa Lo. He wished, idly, that the walk could somehow be prolonged, but his guards stopped him and removed his blindfold. He was in front of a door, one of several in the face of a long shed. He waited, blinking while his vision returned. A guard worked a key into a lock and then swung the door open.

"Stafford," a guard said, "this is your new room." It was a cell, by any name, but the Vietnamese called them rooms and the POWs went along. You lived in a "room," and you had "roommates," almost as if you were back at college.

Stafford stared into the cell, which was illuminated by a single bare bulb hanging from the ceiling by a strand of frayed black wire. The room was much larger than his cell at Hoa Lo. And there were two men standing in the room some distance from the door.

"These are your new roommates. You must obey camp regulations or you will be punished."

The guard began to recite the camp regulations, but Stafford did not listen. He was trying to focus his eyes on the two men in the room. Were they Americans, or was he being put in a cell with Vietnamese prisoners?

The guard finished the litany of regulations against communicating with other prisoners, attempting to escape, bringing contraband into the rooms, and so forth, then motioned for Stafford to step into the cell. He did, and the door closed firmly behind him. He was close enough now to make out the faces of the other two men. They were unmistakably Americans.

Four

STAFFORD'S NEW ROOMMATES were Bob Sawhill and Tom Parrott. The men introduced themselves cautiously — not sure that one or the other wasn't a plant — and were still uneasy when a guard opened the small sliding window in the door and told them to go to bed. They strung their mosquito nets over their bunks — boards the size of a door which rested on a pair of sawhorses. A rice mat went over the surface of the board, and each man had a single blanket.

There was a window in the back wall of the room which had been sealed hastily with bricks and mortar. But outside air and insects came in through gaps in the door frame and through a large opening in the ceiling that looked as if it had been cut as some kind of improvised gun port.

The room seemed alive with insects, but the mosquito nets gave some protection. The single bare bulb burned constantly, so Stafford, Sawhill, and Parrott could look at one another while they talked. They tried to keep their voices low, since loud talk was certain to bring the guards. They spoke with a kind of feverish urgency.

They told one another first who they were. For aviators this meant what rank they held in which service and what type of plane they flew. Bob Sawhill was an air force major, the pilot of an F-4. Tom Parrott, an air force captain, was not a pilot but an F-4 back-seater, an intelligence specialist.

Each man told the story of his shootdown, something every POW would tell over and over again. Some would refine it until, after a couple of years, they were only vaguely aware of the way it had actually happened. For Parrott, Sawhill, and Stafford this was the first chance to give their accounts, and they were true and unembellished. Even so, there was a kind of odd pleasure in telling the story, in being detached enough to describe it in detail.

They talked about the war — what they knew for certain and what they could guess about the way it was going. They were able to agree that it probably would not last much longer. The status of the war was another prime topic of conversation among POWs, the subject uppermost in their minds. Since they could not know with any precision, they speculated endlessly. These three, on this night, had been shot down recently, and while they were flying, the air war had been increasing in intensity almost daily. They did not doubt that the pressure would continue and that North Vietnam would soon buckle. Six months or less. Six months was the magic figure.

Finally they began to talk about their immediate situation and the events between shootdown and the present. The conversation faltered and grew strained as each man tried to find a way to say the same thing.

At last Stafford decided that he would have to say it, that he could not hide what he had done forever, and that if the other two were going to ostracize him, then he would just have to get used to it.

"Listen, you two," he said, "there is something I've got to tell you."

Two gaunt, unshaven faces looked back at him from the shadows beneath the netting, but Stafford could not read anything in their expressions. He felt a surge of shame and hesitated, then decided he had no real choice. He had to tell them and just hope that they would not hold his weakness against him.

"Ah . . . when they asked me questions, and started working me over, I'm afraid I didn't do too well. I mean . . . I gave them a little more than just name, rank, and serial number."

His new roommates looked at him silently; their expressions did not change. It was almost as though they had not heard a word he said, or worse, that they had heard every word and were overwhelmed by his confession of weakness.

"I tried to hold out but . . . well, shit, I just couldn't. They broke me." He felt the hot flush of shame all over again and looked down at the floor to avoid their eyes.

Finally one of them spoke. "You too?" he said. "Well, then, join the fucking club."

The stories poured out, and they were identical in the essentials. All three of them had been tortured and broken. Stafford came close to crying with relief.

Later, near morning, there was a bombing raid, and for some reason the overhead light went out. Either the power had been knocked out or the camp had been intentionally darkened. The three men lay in the blackness and listened to the hard concussion of bombs exploding less than a mile away, feeling the walls of their cell shake. It was plain that they were on the outskirts of Hanoi, not too far from the perimeter of the ten-mile circle inside of which there were no air raids. The raid lasted only a few minutes, and when it was over the light came back on.

In the glare of the light the men saw a spider the size of a man's hand crawling across the wall of the cell. It was easily the largest spider any of them had ever seen. None of them knew what kind of spider it was or whether it was dangerous.

"Well, I'll tell you this," Stafford said after some discussion. "If we have to share space with that sonofabitch, then it's going to be a long goddamned war."

Parrott shook his head and said in a soft Georgia drawl, "Tell yew somethin' else, too. If that sumbitch *bites*, it'll be a short goddamned war."

This struck all of them as wildly, helplessly funny, and they began to laugh. Once they started laughing, none of them could stop. They laughed until it hurt and until they were sure that the noise would bring the guards and punishment, but still they could not stop. When the laughter began to die, one of them would start again, unable to help himself, and the others would follow, until they were all laughing hysterically, tears rolling down their cheeks, arms wrapped around their rib cages, their throats aching, their lungs begging for air. They laughed for what seemed like hours. Stafford was sure that he had never laughed so long and so hard in his entire life. Finally he stopped, his side aching from the broken ribs. He fell into the first thing resembling restful sleep that he had experienced in a long time.

In the morning the three men were awakened by a gong. They began talking again, speculating about just what was next. What was the significance of the fact that they had been moved into this camp and given roommates? It had to *mean* something.

Probably, they agreed, the worst was over. They had been tortured for what could be wrung out of them, and while they hadn't resisted according to the line laid down in survival training, they had done well enough that the Vietnamese knew they were not prime material for defectors or collaborators. From now on, they assured one another, it would be a matter of marking time. Later in the morning they would be let out for exercise. They would visit with any other prisoners who might be at the camp. Maybe there would be a volleyball game.

This was the first of countless cycles of hope and disillusionment.

Two or three hours after the gong had awakened them, a key turned in the door. Guards motioned for the men to put their buckets — "shit buckets" they were universally called by POWs — outside the door. Sawhill and Parrott carried them. They refused Stafford's offer of help, pointing to his broken arm.

A few minutes later they heard someone come by the cell door, stop, and pick up the buckets. They looked through the cracks around the door and saw that the man collecting the buckets was another American. A few minutes later the buckets were returned and the key turned in the lock. A guard told them to take the buckets back in the cell.

The door closed and the lock turned.

"Volleyball must be later," Parrott said.

Guards came around in the middle of the morning with breakfast: pumpkin soup dipped from a large tub. Each man was given a bowl. They sat and began slowly eating the soup, trying to make the meal last. The guards returned before they were finished and collected the bowls. The door closed and the lock turned again.

They talked and they waited. Nothing happened until midafternoon, when the guards returned with more pumpkin soup and some small loaves of bread. The bread was full of weevils. Parrott looked up after taking a bite and said, "Goddamn, this bread is eating *me*." Still, they ate hastily and finished before the guards returned.

Nothing further happened that day until a guard came by after sundown and told them to get under their nets and go to sleep.

Simply having someone to talk with for the first time since they had been shot down made the emptiness of the day seem bearable, and they still believed that, sooner or later, the routine would change and become something like what they knew from reading about pilots captured in World War II. Volleyball still seemed possible.

The routine did not change the next day, or any day that week, except for the two occasions when each man was led from the cell to a small latrine area to wash with tepid water dipped from a large cistern. He was given a bar of abrasively strong lye soap for himself and his clothes and a dull communal safety razor to use on his face. This trip to the latrine generally took about fifteen minutes.

To fill the long, empty stretches, the three men would watch through the open gun port to see if they could gauge time by the passage of the sun and the shadows it left on the wall. They studied the layout of the camp through the gaps around the door. It was evidently some sort of old estate. There was a large main building with a wide front porch and columns, its white paint bleached by the sun. Surrounding the main building, which they called, inevitably, the Big House, there were rows of sheds which had been divided into small rooms like the one they occupied. These, they decided, had been the laborers' quarters. There were large oaks and flame trees on the grounds as well as small garden plots, which the guards tended and where the pumpkins and the greens that went into their soup were grown.

Among the POWs every camp in Vietnam had a name. There was the Hanoi Hilton, Alcatraz, the Zoo, and Dogpatch. This camp was the Plantation.

Stafford and his roommates tried to look through cracks and gaps in the walls to see if there were men in the cells adjacent to theirs. As far as they could tell, those cells were empty. But they knew that other Americans were being held in the camp. They saw them as they were taken from other cells down to the latrine to bathe, wash their clothes, and shave. They saw them collecting buckets in the morning. And they watched when one would be led, ominously, up to the Big House for reasons they could only guess at.

They did not recognize any of these other Americans, and they had no way of communicating with them to find out who they were, how long they had been there, when they had been shot down, and, most important, what they knew about how the war was going.

They were reduced to what they could make of life in their barren room, from days in which there were only four events: the collecting of the buckets, morning soup, afternoon soup, and at night a broadcast of war news — heavily propagandized — by a series of female announcers known collectively as "Hanoi Hannah."

So they worked at keeping the room and themselves clean, since they were already suffering from skin rashes, dysentery, and, in Stafford's case, a persistent hacking cough. They had no reading or writing materials, no cards, nothing to fill the time except conversation. So they talked, endlessly.

At first the talk was pointless and random. But after three or four weeks they realized that, if they were going to hold on to their sanity through conversation, they needed to give it some structure and discipline.

Bob Sawhill made his talk professionally compelling. He was a bachelor, the son of schoolteachers, and something of a gentleman fighter pilot. He knew his airplane and could talk about it in detail. So he talked about the F-4, which Stafford had never flown, and he talked about the restaurants where he had taken his dates, the kinds of cigars he liked to smoke and the whiskey he liked to drink. As he lost weight on the diet of pumpkin soup and bread, he would put his hand over his diminishing belly and say, mournfully, "I invested sixty thousand dollars in this gut, and now look at it."

Stafford found himself talking about his childhood, which had been spent, first, with a grandfather he loved on a farm near Rocky Mount, North Carolina, and then with a stepfather he respected on the Eastern Shore of Maryland. His stepfather was the publisher of a small, influential newspaper and, in his time, had done some ghostwriting for Franklin Roosevelt. This was good material in a cell outside of Hanoi.

Even better was Stafford's story about the time he had met Billy Rose, the Broadway showman, whose column "Pitching Horseshoes" appeared in his stepfather's paper. When Stafford was fourteen he had written to Rose, telling him how much he enjoyed the column. Rose wrote back to Stafford's stepfather inviting the boy to join him in Manhattan as his guest for lunch and an afternoon at the theater. Stafford and his mother took the train to New York and had lunch with Rose at the Diamond Horseshoe, then saw Mary Martin and Ezio Pinza in *South Pacific*.

It was a story that Stafford could have told at the officers' club — if the occasion had come up — in less than five minutes. Any longer and he would have bored his audience blind. But under these conditions a synopsis was unacceptable. Sawhill and Parrott wanted to hear it all.

"Where did you catch the train, Al?"

"What line was it?"

"Did you have a Pullman?"

"What hotel did you stay in?"

"What did you have for lunch?"

Simple recall became a discipline, and Stafford found himself concentrating, working to get the details right and to provide enough of them so that a story was completely fleshed out and took a good chunk of time to tell. He would feel a strange sense of accomplishment whenever he told a story, talking his way through something that had happened over fifteen years earlier; then the key would suddenly turn in the door and the guard would be there with the soup. He would eat with an extra measure of satisfaction. Sometimes he actually felt a kind of physical fatigue from the effort of getting the story right.

For Stafford and Sawhill, storytelling was hard work. Tom Parrott, by contrast, simply had a gift. He was a natural, a born talker. He had the rural southerner's fondness for words and stories and the ability to use them to fill long, vacant stretches of time. He spoke in a slow, soft drawl that was almost musical in its capacity to diminish his listeners' ordinary, anxious sense of time. In their cell at Plantation, Sawhill and Stafford would sit on their bunks or on the floor, leaning against the crumbling wall, hour after hour, listening as Parrott's stories rolled on.

Parrott had been brought up in Dalton, Georgia, where his family owned and operated a motel and restaurant. He could talk about the most trivial episode from his childhood and recall detail down to the quality of the heat on the day he first took a girl for a drive in a car. He recreated and populated the entire town of Dalton for his audience of two, so that Stafford and Sawhill began to recognize people by name and to anticipate just how they would act in one of Parrott's developing narratives. There was a familiar undercurrent to the life of Parrott's small town; it recalled *Peyton Place*. Things were not always as tranquil as they appeared on the surface in Dalton. Envy, greed, malice, and especially sex motivated people in ways that were both plausible and fascinating. Sawhill and Stafford began to feel that they knew the red-dirt town of Dalton and its people far better than they had ever known any of the towns where they had lived.

One morning Parrott began talking about how he had bought his first car, a Dodge. The first thing he did with that car was change the tires.

"Why in the hell did you do that, Tom? Brand-new tires. What was wrong with them?"

"They might have been brand new, but I just got rid of those rascals, and you know why?"

"No."

"Because they weren't Generals. Your General tire, now,

is the finest tire that money can buy. There is no tire, any-where, that can even come close to your General. I'd rather have a set of used Generals than a set of anything else brand new. There just isn't any comparison."

And then he set off on a long description of buying his new set of General tires and taking them back to the motel, where he parked the car out back and proceeded to get out the jack and raise the car so that he could get at one of those original, inferior tires, remove the lug nuts, pull the tire off, and replace it with one of those fine Generals, tightening the lug nut down, going around the tire and taking a turn or two on each lug nut so they tightened down even, then lowering the car and moving the jack around to the next tire and doing it again, in exactly the same way.

Parrott was to tell this story — and the others from his stock — for another five years, to dozens of different room-mates, most of whom still think of him whenever they see an ad in the paper for General tires.

For three months Stafford, Sawhill, and Parrott left their cell only to bathe. They were awakened every morning by the gong, fed pumpkin soup twice a day, and told when to lower their nets and go to bed on their boards and rice mats. They had no way of knowing how long this regimen would last. Within the space of a single thought they could imagine six more months or twenty years.

There were times when the stories wore thin and the room would be quiet and still except for the small, random sounds made by insects. Each man had to find a way to fill these intervals. It was Parrott's nature to pull his blanket over his head and sleep or daydream. Sawhill would sit quietly and think, working out solutions to school problems the way he had when he was growing up and his parents were oversee-ing his homework. Stafford paced.

He had always been physically restless, bothered by an itch that he relieved by driving or flying. When he was stateside, he would spend weekends on the road or, better, take a plane out to get some cross-country hours. So in Plantation he paced the cell, back and forth, eight steps each way, turning right and then left, back and forth, working off the restlessness. He walked fast, with a kind of desperation, mile after mile, until he wore sores on his feet around the straps of his sandals.

One day, while Stafford was walking, Sawhill looked up from the corner where he was sitting, absorbed in his thoughts, and said, "Goddammit, Al, do you have to *pace* all the time? Can't you just relax?"

Stafford stopped abruptly, like a dog whose leash has suddenly been pulled tight. It was the first hostile note in the three months they had been in the room together. There was a long, tense interval, during which Stafford tried to think of something to say. He and Sawhill stared at each other in silence.

Finally, Stafford spoke hesitantly. "I didn't know it bothered you. I'm sorry."

"It's all right," Sawhill said. The edge had gone off his voice. "Just not all the time, okay?"

"Sure, Bob. I'll try to keep it down."

Stafford sat and leaned against the wall. Nothing more was said.

Tension was inevitable in close, uncertain confinement with absolutely nothing to do — no diversions of any kind except the sound of another man's voice and the arrival of the monotonous pumpkin soup. Inevitable and dangerous. To a POW a roommate was a lifeboat. In solitary a man would sink into a sea of despair. Bad as it was to be confined in a barren room with two other men and absolutely no privacy even when you sat on the bucket, being alone in that room would be immeasurably worse. In solitary Stafford had hit what he was sure was the absolute bottom. With roommates he had, in some measure, come back to life.

There was no way a man could anticipate or prepare for the intimacy he would experience with another man — or men — in a cell in Hanoi. At the farthest extreme, men nursed one another through sickness and injuries that would otherwise have been fatal. They cleaned up after one another, fed one another, comforted one another after torture sessions or in times when there didn't seem to be any point whatsoever in living.

But they also grew sick to death of one another's company. To the point, occasionally, of not speaking for months at a time and even fighting with fists and feet, two men trying physically to destroy each other. One fight lasted for days. The men traded punches until they were both too tired and weak to fight anymore and could only sit in opposite corners of the cell and glare at each other through swollen, bloody eyes. Then, when they had their strength back, they would begin pounding on each other again. Everyone in the camp knew, could hear the sounds of the fight, but no one could do anything about it, and the guards let it go on until the two men were finally too worn down to keep on fighting. For months afterwards they shared the cell in hostile silence, like two caged animals, until they were finally separated.

In another case a man let out of his cell for a bath refused to go back in until he was given a new roommate or put in solitary. He was taken to the Big House, to the office of the camp commander, where he repeated his demands. He was prepared to go through the ropes, *anything*, before he would go back and share a cell with that miserable sonofabitch. This was an utterly new and bewildering experience for the camp commander, and he was uncharacteristically accommodating. He tried to explain that it was administratively impossible, at the moment, to make a change. The American remained firm. He would go in the ropes before he went back to that cell.

The camp commander could not give in to prisoner demands. That would destroy camp discipline and lose him too much face. But he did make a promise to the American. If he would go back to his cell, peaceably, then in a few days, maybe a week or two, there would be a reorganization of the camp — one was being planned — and then he could have a new roommate.

Fair enough, the POW said. It was by far the best he could hope for. He returned to his cell and a couple of weeks later was moved to another. When he told his astounded new roommate about the episode, he said, grimly, that it was a long gamble but worth the risk.

"I'd have done anything to get out of there," he said. "Any fucking thing at all."

But most men, by far, found ways to keep from getting to this point. That was part of the hard work of being a POW, of surviving in an impossible situation. Later in the war one of Stafford's roommates told him about the first man he had shared a cell with in Hanoi — a man who was almost his exact opposite, someone he had every reason to dislike and maybe even hate. Whereas he was a quiet, reserved, and almost gentle product of rural Indiana, he told Stafford, his roommate was a city kid, Italian, and very tightly wrapped. "A feisty guy, Al. Very, very feisty."

His roommate was also a career pilot, a career military man and hard nosed about it; by contrast, he was still, in his mind, a civilian, a reserve lieutenant not long out of flight training. He had been on his eighteenth mission when he was shot down, but he had not even finished unpacking and barely knew his way around the base back in Thailand when he was bagged.

Still, the two of them had been thrown together, and while

they tried to make the best of the situation and keep it military, it was hard. "I mean really *hard,* Al. On top of everything else, this guy and I couldn't get along. And even when we weren't saying anything to get on each other's nerves, he'd do these things that would just drive me up the wall. For one thing, he had this habit of gagging when he brushed his teeth, and he was always brushing his teeth for some reason. Every time, this little gagging noise would come out of his throat, and after a while it got to where I wanted to strangle him every time I heard it.

"But there was another thing even worse than that. He liked to pace, same as you, only when he walked his ankle would pop. I don't know what it was: maybe he hurt the ankle when he ejected. But whatever it was, the goddamned thing made this little *pop* every time he took a step. And he walked all day long. It was worse than the worst dripping faucet ever.

"I think we probably would have killed each other if they'd just left us alone in there. I mean, the air was getting really thick. But one day the gooks came for him for some reason. He'd given a guard some shit on the way to the shower or something, I don't know. But they kept him for a long time — seems like it was a couple of weeks — and they really worked him over. Guys heard him screaming and told me about it through the wall.

"I sat there and worried about him and I realized that if they killed him, I'd actually miss the guy. I just kept thinking about him and worrying about him and feeling like shit because I couldn't do anything to help him. Finally, they brought him back and he was really a mess. Couldn't do anything for himself, just lay in his bunk. So I fed him and washed him and after a few days he came around. We talked about things a little and said, 'You know, we've got to make sure we don't let the chicken-shit stuff get between us because we really need each other.' And we worked things out.

"We were in that cell for another six or eight months, anyway, and we never had any more trouble. And I'll tell you what, I still feel close to the guy. Real close."

The shadow of the pacing episode passed. Stafford, Sawhill, and Parrott continued to tell stories and to speculate on the progress of the war. Stafford tried to keep his pacing down. Sawhill tried not to let it get to him. Parrott slept or told stories.

Then, after they had been together for three months, a guard opened the door and impatiently signaled for Stafford and Sawhill to roll up their gear and follow him. They said good-bye to Parrott and left the cell.

The guard led them up to the Big House to the camp commander's office. Two other POWs were already there, sitting on stools, with their gear bundled on their laps. At first Stafford did not recognize either of the men. They just looked dirty and whipped.

Stafford and Sawhill were told to sit, and the camp commander explained that they were moving into a new room and that these men would be their roommates. The commander gave the men's names. When he heard the name Chauncey, Stafford was shocked. He looked at the man next to him. It was almost impossible to believe that this gaunt, hollowed-out man was the same Arv Chauncey he had known back in flight training in Pensacola a thousand years ago. Chauncey was tall, maybe six-four, and he'd been big, strong, and imposing. Now you could see his bones. He must have lost a hundred pounds, Stafford thought, and he looked brittle and frail, like a starving old man.

Stafford knew that he probably looked as bad as, or worse than, Chauncey. The realization filled him with a sickening sense of dread. If it was that bad after less than six months, he thought, then he couldn't possibly make it for another six. The war had to end soon or he would be dead.

Five

STAFFORD and the other three men were led from the Big House to a large room at the end of a long shed that had been broken up into several cells. When the door closed behind them, they went through the ritual of introductions, including a complete military biography, which was important in order to establish seniority within the room and the camp. Senior ranking officer in the room — and, as it turned out, in all of Plantation — was Richard Stratton. He was also one of the most celebrated, and controversial, figures of the war.

Stratton's A-4 had gone down on January 5, 1967, when his engine ingested pieces of obsolete rockets that had malfunctioned when he had fired them at some pontoon bridges. He was the first pilot downed after one of the bombing halts periodically ordered by the Johnson administration as an overture to peace talks. Like the others, this cease-fire had failed, and when the planes resumed their attacks, the bombing campaign became a matter of even greater controversy — within the military, among American voters, and in the international community.

The North Vietnamese were alert to the controversy and the possibilities it afforded them. Outsiders, especially from Iron Curtain and neutral nations, had been allowed in to document the civilian destruction and loss of life caused by American air raids. At the moment when Stratton was captured, Harrison Salisbury of the *New York Times*, the first American reporter with establishment credentials to visit North Vietnam, was in the country researching articles that would substantially back the North Vietnamese claims and repudiate those of the Johnson administration, which insisted that American planes were hitting only hard military targets — concrete and steel. Salisbury's dispatches caused a sensation when they appeared and eventually earned a controversial Pulitzer Prize for the *Times*.

Perhaps because the propaganda war seemed so clearly to be going their way, the North Vietnamese leadership decided to produce a confession from one of the captured "air pirates," in which he would acknowledge bombing civilian targets for the purpose of terrorizing the population. Richard Stratton was the pilot who would be made to confess.

He spent hours in the ropes. His wrists were so badly cut, and the cuts became so seriously infected, that Stratton nearly lost his arm. He was promised medical attention if he confessed. Inevitably, he did.

The confession was pieced together from several interviews. Stratton read the final version from a script and was tape-recorded. The tape was played at a press conference for visiting journalists, including a photographer on assignment from *Life* magazine. When the tape had played through, Stratton was marched in front of the audience for pictures. He had been ordered to make no statement and answer no questions — the North Vietnamese did not trust him to remain docile. He was to bow, slightly, to the people in the room and let them take his picture. Nothing more.

But while he was waiting to step out on stage, Stratton listened to the tape of his confession with rising dismay. He had tried to read the words in a mechanical, uninflected voice so that anyone listening would realize he was speaking under some form of duress. But as he listened, he realized that his dead monotone might not be enough to convey this fact.

So when he stepped out on the stage and was told by one of his captors to bow, Stratton did not merely nod his head politely and deferentially as he'd been told to do. Instead, he bowed deeply from the waist. Then he turned ninety degrees and bowed again. Another turn, another bow. And a fourth. Throughout this sequence of abject, mechanical bows, Stratton's remote and empty expression never changed. He looked like a man who had been stripped of his will and then crudely reprogrammed. His behavior recalled the most lurid accounts of brainwashing, and it was horrifying to those who witnessed the performance and those who saw the photographs, later, in *Life*.

This was the first widely distributed evidence that the North Vietnamese were not treating the POWs humanely as they claimed, and as their supporters had reported. But in fact the U.S. government had uncovered similar evidence, a few months earlier, when a group of POWs had been forced to sit for an interview with a Japanese television crew, and Jeremiah Denton, a very early shootdown, had blinked his eyes to spell out T-O-R-T-U-R-E in Morse code. The film was studied by American intelligence analysts, but the administration chose not to make an issue of the treatment of POWs. Since the North Vietnamese would not allow visits by the International Red Cross or any other neutral agency to conduct independent examinations of the camps, there was virtually no evidence regarding treatment of prisoners. Nothing except for that which was put out or staged by the North Vietnamese — until Stratton was seized with the inspiration to bow like a brainwashed character from *The Manchurian Candidate*.

*

Stratton had been a prisoner for a little more than a year now. It had been nine months since the shocking bowing performance, almost six since he had arrived at Plantation. He was an old hand. So was Chauncey, who had also been one of the first men held in Plantation. He and Stratton had known each other, although this was the first time they had been in a room together.

"Arv," Stratton said when the introductions were complete and it was established that he was senior, "you get on the wall and see if you can find out who else is here. I want to know if I'm SRO in the camp."

"Roger," Chauncey said and stepped up close to the wall that was common with the next cell, knelt, and began rapping on the wall with his knuckle. After a minute or two he stopped and put his ear close to the wall where a softer rapping sound came through from the other side. As Chauncey concentrated on the sounds, which seemed to have no rhythm and no point, he moved his lips like a child learning to read.

The rapping stopped.

"We've still got the Thundering Herd next door," he said. "And next to them, it's Shively, Crecca, Abbott, Mechenbier, and Torquelson. They're still trying to establish comm. with the next room."

"Okay. Tell them I want to know who is in that room ASAP. Names and date of rank."

"Roger." Chauncey began knocking on the wall with his knuckle. While he was formulating this message, a single hard rap, louder than any of the tapping, came through the wall of the next cell. Chauncey quickly stood up and stepped back from the wall. A second or two later the sliding window in the cell door opened and the face of a guard appeared there. He studied the four men for a minute, then closed the window without a word. Stratton stepped to the door and looked through a crack around the frame. A minute later he turned to Chauncey.

"Clear," he said.

Chauncey went back to the wall, knelt, and began his rapid tapping.

Sawhill and Stafford looked at each other, mystified, then at Stratton.

"What the hell *is* this?"

"We've got a code," Stratton said. And then he explained the tap code, the POWs' life line.

At all of the POW camps in North Vietnam communication between prisoners was strictly forbidden. A man could safely talk to his roommates, if he did not get too loud, but he could not shout through walls or windows or leave messages or try in any other way to make contact with the other prisoners in the camp. To try was to risk punishment. Men were thrown in solitary, locked in irons, hung in ropes, and beaten when they were caught communicating.

Still, it was worth the risk, since communication was the foundation of any kind of resistance. The senior man had to get his orders out to everyone in the camp, and everyone had to be tied in. Three men alone in a room were still not part of a unified resistance.

But with the tap code, they could be.

The principle is ancient, at least as old as Greek civilization. In modern dress it appears in Arthur Koestler's descriptions of life in the Soviet Gulag in his novel *Darkness at Noon*. POWs believed that the code had been invented by an air force captain named Smitty Harris, who had come up with it while he was at survival school and remembered it in Hoa Lo, after he was shot down.

While the POWs may have been wrong about the origins of the tap code, no group in history ever employed it more successfully or enthusiastically. Learning the code was like getting a telephone: it opened a world.

Stratton drew a box on the concrete floor, using a piece of chipped brick for chalk. He divided the larger box into smaller boxes and then wrote the letters of the alphabet in the smaller boxes. When he finished, the grid looked like this:

A	B	C	D	E
F	G	H	I	J
L	M	N	O	P
Q	R	S	T	U
V	W	X	Y	Z

The letter *G* could be substituted for *K*, Stratton explained, and the code was read like the coordinates on a map — top down and left to right. For example, the letter *M* would be three down and two across. To transmit an *M* through the wall, then, a prisoner would tap three times, pause, then tap twice.

"You figure out what you want to say," Stratton explained, "and then you try to get it down to the bare minimum number of words. Use as many abbreviations as you can. Then you get the attention of the guy on the other wall and tap it through. It's slow at first, but you get to where it's almost as fast as talking. Chauncey here is a first-rate communicator. Smooth and fast. But it is hell on the knuckles."

Chauncey showed the new men his bleeding calluses. "I use this now," he said, and held up a small nail that he had pried from the wall. He used the nail like a telegraph key.

"Whenever we have someone on the wall, which is almost all of the time," Stratton said, "we also have someone clearing. That was the heavy thud you heard on the wall. The guards are up and down this line of cells all day long. If they look in and catch you on the wall, they will haul your ass up to the Big House and start asking you about escape plans and telling you to write a letter of apology to the camp commander. You don't want to wind up in the ropes for tapping on the wall."

Stratton and Sawhill tried the tap code and found it slow and clumsy. It was frustrating to watch Chauncey effortlessly rap out his messages with the little nail.

"Takes time," he said. "And if you think this is bad, try to imagine what it would be like if you didn't have someone in your cell to explain it to you. Picture learning this baby when you are in a cell by yourself and someone on your wall knows it."

That, Stafford said, sounded impossible.

Happened a lot, Chauncey said, and he explained how it was done. A man who knew the code simply pounded on the wall until he got a response. He might beat out the familiar rhythm of "shave and a haircut" until the man on the other side came back with "two bits." Once that happened, they were in communication. Then the tedious business of establishing a language began. The first man would tap once, then pause, tap twice, then pause, tap three times, then pause . . . and so on, until he reached twenty-six. Then he would do it again.

Eventually the other man would understand that the twenty-six taps represented the alphabet. *A* was one, *B* was two, and so on.

When this had been established, a few messages would be transmitted. The men would exchange names, perhaps, and shootdown dates. It was exceedingly slow and tedious, but it established the link and the rudiments of the method.

Then the man who knew the code would tap out the message: MAKE A MATRIX. Next, he would tell the other man to fill in the alphabet. Eventually, using the first code, he would have explained the much shorter, more efficient system.

"Here at Plantation," Chauncey said, "we've got everyone tied in."

Since Stratton was senior in the camp, the wall of his cell — called Warehouse One because it was the first in the line of cells hastily partitioned in the old shed — was alive with the sound of messages going out and coming in. Chauncey did most of the tapping, since he was fast and agile with the code. The primary objective of communication among POWs was to learn who was being held in the camp, specifically, and in North Vietnam in general. Plantation was one of several camps, and men were moved around frequently and randomly. Stratton wanted names.

While Chauncey tapped and then listened to the incoming messages, one of the other men would stand next to him and memorize the names as they came through the wall. The others would stand at the door and watch for guards through the crack.

In addition to acquiring names, which they memorized like a mantra, the men used the tap code to keep other prisoners informed when someone was taken from his cell up to the Big House for interrogation, which the POWs called quizzes.

SHIVELY TO BGHS FR QZ, a message might read.

When a man was returned to his cell after several hours, or days, in the Big House, he would be debriefed. What had the interrogators wanted? What had he given them? How rough had they been?

SHIVELY SAYS QZ FOR BMBING TACTICS. REFSD TO TALK. NO ROPES.

When a new prisoner appeared in the camp, the other POWs attempted to make contact and establish communication as quickly as possible. They wanted the name first.

NEW SHTDWN IS LT ED MILLER USN. FLYING F-8 PHOTO FRM BON HOMME RICHARD. NO SERIOUS INJRY.

The date of the new man's shootdown would be quickly established, and he would be extensively debriefed for any news on the subject uppermost in every POW's mind: the progress, if any, of the war. Inevitably, the new man would report that the pressure was increasing and the Vietnamese would not be able to hold out much longer. Six months was the normal prediction for the probable length of hostilities. For more than seven years the men heard, every few days, that the war would be over in another six months.

After he had reported what he knew about the progress of the war, a new man would be pumped for anything about the world outside. Aviators, who were normally not avid newspaper readers, could not get enough news once they had been shot down. They were starved for data about life "in the World," and devoured any information a new man could give them. If he didn't produce, they would tap furiously, telling him, goddammit, to try harder. Who had won the Indianapolis 500? The Super Bowl? For men who were captured before 1966, the existence of this "Super Bowl" required explanation. Others tapped out questions that were equally difficult at a time when, back in the States, something called the Summer of Love had just ended.

EXPLAIN HIPPIE.

So the tap code was invaluable. It broke the wall of isolation and gave the POWs a sense that they were once again part of a group with a common purpose, even if that objective was something as small as frustrating their captors and putting together a good list of names. But by tapping out their names on a wall, they found out who they were and then what they could do to help one another. The tap code gave them a way to reach out to a man who was sick or injured or had been badly beaten and bent in the ropes and was near the end of his resources, ready to quit or even to die. The tap code was the only means for transmitting the fundamental, reassuring message: "Hang in there. We're with you."

There were times when the tap code gave the POWs a way to take back a crucial part of their identity, to put on the irreverent and defiant face that fighter pilots have always tried to show the world. It was a pilot, dying of his wounds, who, when he was asked, "Does it hurt?" is supposed to have answered, "Only when I laugh."

From Stafford's new cell, at the end of a long shed and on a corner of the courtyard, he and his roommates could observe traffic in and out of the Big House. One day a prisoner was taken from his cell for interrogation, and for days Stafford and the others watched, waiting for him to be returned. When he was finally led out of the Big House, the man was plainly in bad shape. He had been beaten and hung in the ropes, and now he staggered across the courtyard, bloody and uncomprehending, to an empty cell where he was locked up alone. While he was still lying on the floor of his dark cell, too weak even to sit or to lie on his bunk, he heard the soft, steady tapping of words coming through the wall. He crawled closer, so he could make out the letters, and through a red blur of pain, he counted out the taps and transposed them to letters and then words, putting it all into a message:

RESEARCH PROVES THAT NINETY NINE PRCNT OF POWS JAC OFF. WE NEED YOUR HELP TO MAKE IT ONE HUNDRED PRCNT.

Years later the man would say that message had probably saved his sanity, if not his life.

That was the spirit of much of what went through the walls. Self-pity and bitching were unacceptable, according to the unofficial communications protocol. You tried for the stoic "Only when I laugh" posture whenever possible, and sometimes you had to reach. An apotheosis of sorts was achieved one evening when Al Stafford began to cough uncontrollably. He had been ill for days and assumed he had some kind of respiratory problem and there was nothing for it. No drugs. Certainly no chicken soup. It was winter, and the leaky, unheated cells were cold. The men had only their thin prison uniforms and a single blanket, which they huddled beneath day and night.

Stafford's coughing grew worse and worse until, finally, he realized that he was gagging on something lodged in the back of his throat. The obstruction actually seemed to be growing; it felt as if it was slowly choking off the airway. Alarmed, Stafford reached down his throat with his fingers, trying to locate whatever it was that was choking him. His fingers closed around something that felt warm and fleshy, and he began to pull. It took a while, but he finally removed the obstruction — a wiggling six-inch worm. Many of the men had become infected with parasitic worms, although it was rare to pass them orally. Stafford had probably picked his up when he drank water from the cistern, after his first interrogation in the Green Knobby Room.

Chauncey got on the wall:

CONGRATULATIONS TO LTCDR AL STAFFORD WHO GAVE BIRTH AT 1630 HRS TO A SIX INCH FIVE OUNCE WORM. BOTH STAFFORD AND WORM DOING FINE.

There was solace in humor, however bleak. But the POWs also employed the tap code to wish one another Merry Christmas and to pray. Some men who had been marginally religious before they were shot down would fall back increasingly on the scraps of Bible verse they could remember from Sunday school or the days of mandatory chapel at the various service academies. On Sunday mornings one of the men would hold a form of worship service, tapping out the prayers and his sermon.

Most POWs were about as devout as could be expected of fighter pilots. Stafford had considered himself agnostic, when he thought about it at all, before he was shot down. Even during the worst of his experiences during interrogation and torture, he had never felt the stirrings of a religious conversion. But like all of the other POWs, when he tapped out the last message of the day, he would close with the letters GBU CUL. This was the POW signature. It translated, simply, as "God bless you; see you later."

With time, that sequence of sounds became a kind of litany or chant, like the first few melancholy notes of the bugle call taps. Prisoners kneeling next to a dirty stone wall would hear the sequence and, for a few moments, experience a feeling of peace.

Six

THE PRISONERS in Plantation, like the rest of the American military, were unaware of the Vietnamese plans and preparations during the winter of 1967–68. They would all be horribly surprised when the Vietcong and North Vietnamese launched attacks all over South Vietnam on January 30, 1968, the first day of a truce that had been declared in order to observe Tet, the lunar new year and the most important Vietnamese holiday.

The North Vietnamese had been increasingly bold and aggressive in the weeks leading up to Tet. First, they had engaged the marines along the demilitarized zone with heavy artillery and infantry assaults. Next, they attacked U.S. army units in strength around Dakto in the central highlands of South Vietnam. And then, in what looked, superficially, like a repeat of their critical battle with the French at Dien Bien Phu, the North Vietnamese laid siege to the marine base at Khesanh, not far from the Laotian border in the extreme northwest corner of South Vietnam. Finally, on the first day of the Tet cease-fire, they attacked cities all over South Vietnam, including Saigon, where sappers actually penetrated the U.S. embassy, symbolic nerve center of the American war effort.

The North Vietnamese were making a supreme push,

militarily and politically, stretching their resources to the limit in order to press this offensive. The Americans escalated in turn, intensifying the air war in order to disrupt supplies to the South and break the morale of the people in North Vietnam. Plantation was located along the run-in line for bombing attacks on one of the main bridges in Hanoi. The POWs could hear the planes going over when they made their attacks, and sometimes range errors resulted in near misses that shook the walls and left dust drifting in the close air of the cells.

Stafford and Chauncey were arguing one day over some minor issue, but confinement and the smell of the bucket and hunger had raised the tension so that they were on the verge of swinging. Suddenly they hated each other. Hated the way the other man talked, the stories he told, the way he coughed and scratched and talked all the goddamned time about his wife.

As they were standing there a foot apart, each waiting for the other man to swing, the planes came roaring in and the bombs fell in a string that seemed to uncoil toward the spot where they stood. The concussion shook the camp, and everyone dove for the flimsy protection of the walls and the boards the prisoners used for beds. When the bombs had stopped falling and the air was full of dust, Chauncey and Stafford realized they were holding hands and praying together.

"Kind of hard to stay mad after that," Stafford said.

They went back to work, clearing and tapping, and never quarreled again.

As the war grew in ferocity, the mood inside Plantation and the other camps grew increasingly grim. There was an implacable all-or-nothing spirit in the air which the POWs experienced as increased, unremitting pressure to collaborate.

New shootdowns were broken on the day they were captured. Resisters were left in irons, bent in the ropes, or thrown in solitary in order to extract confessions or, simply, to show the other prisoners what could happen to them if they did not cooperate. The struggle in the camps took on an extra measure of desperation, and many of the POWs began to suspect they might not survive. To men who had been in captivity for two or three years and could make comparisons, these were the worst days yet. By far.

In addition to the extra measure of fear and cruelty, the POWs suffered, more than ever, fundamental physical deprivation. They were cold, sick, and very hungry. Winters are surprisingly cold in North Vietnam, and this was one of the coldest. There was no heat in the cells, only the warmth a man could trap in the folds of a single thin blanket. When he got sick, there was no medicine. And the rations, which were always insufficient, became more meager than ever. Perhaps the bombing was cutting off supplies or the food that was available was going to the troops fighting in the South. Whatever the reason, for 180 consecutive days the men in Plantation ate soup. Two bowls a day. Pumpkin, usually, but on the worst days the soup was made from water and a few sprigs of parsley, not even enough to color it or give it any flavor beyond a kind of bitterness that seemed to dry up a man's mouth like a taste of alum. Eating it made them long to see pumpkin soup again, and those small loaves of bread that were ridden with weevils.

Food became an obsession. It was the first thing a man would think about when he was not passing messages through the walls or memorizing names or keeping watch on the courtyard, clearing for whoever was on the wall. His mouth would water, his stomach would ache, and his knees would go liquid from hunger.

As much as they thought about food, it was impossible for

the POWs not to talk about it. But talking about food required a kind of discipline. If you talked about it all the time, or at the wrong times, it merely made the hunger worse. Oddly, if you talked about it at the right time, it seemed to make the pumpkin soup more filling.

So an hour or so before the bucket of soup was brought around to the cell doors, the four men in Warehouse One would begin to talk about food, about the memorable meals they had eaten and the meals they would eat when they got home, any day now.

"Arv," Stafford would say, when the time for soup was at hand, "I told you about how I grew up on a farm in North Carolina, didn't I?"

"Sure, Al."

"Well, did I tell you about how my grandmother would use the squirrels I'd shoot with my .22?"

"No."

"She was a great cook, my grandmother. And one of her specialties was Brunswick stew. She'd start with some chicken stock. We had chickens on the place. In fact, one of my jobs was to kill the chickens when my grandmother needed one for the pot. She always had some chicken stock handy.

"So, she'd get that simmering and she'd start adding to it. Potatoes and corn and lima beans. Scraps of chicken. Then she'd add the meat from the squirrels I'd shot. She'd cover the pot and let it simmer all afternoon while she baked up some biscuits. You could smell that stew simmering and those biscuits baking all over the house. By supper time I'd be so hungry I would have eaten those squirrels raw."

"God that sounds good."

"It was. And it was the squirrel that made the difference. If you made Brunswick stew with just chicken, the way a lot of people do, it was all right, but it tasted kind of bland, you know. Like chicken soup that somebody had tried to fancy up a little. But that squirrel gave it a kind of texture, you know. It was dark meat. Rich tasting without being too strong or gamy. It made that Brunswick stew stand up and talk to you."

"Al, when we get home, I'm going with you to your grandmother's house for some of that Brunswick stew."

"I want you to. I just hope I still know how to find the squirrels. It isn't right without squirrel."

"Al, we'll find the squirrels."

If he timed it right, the pumpkin soup would arrive just as he finished his story. Then, as the men drank the thin broth, they would imagine themselves at a big country table in a farmhouse, eating thick Brunswick stew and fresh-baked biscuits.

Sometimes they would imagine themselves eating at a restaurant, sitting around a table with clean linen and polished crystal, with a waiter standing by to take their orders. Drinks first. Then appetizers. A salad. Main course. Dessert and coffee. Cigars.

Each man would take the others to his favorite restaurant. The Mark Hopkins in San Francisco. Jimmy's in Boston. Blackie's House of Beef in Washington, D.C. They would strain to recall every detail of the decor, the way the bartender dressed, the weight of the silverware, the quality of the light, the way the waiter served, the dishes on the dessert tray.

They also talked about cooking. The best way to grill a steak. Was it better to boil or broil a lobster? What was the *right* way to rig a New England clambake, roast oysters, fry chicken? It was almost as though they had developed an appetite for information, data, about food, which they could satisfy to compensate for the other, fundamental hunger that was appeased only by pumpkin soup, at best, and parsley-flavored water at worst. They lost weight drastically, but they never seemed to reach that point where they lost all interest in food, the point at which a man begins to die of starvation. They never stopped being hungry.

If the Vietnamese were cutting their rations, it did not mean they were neglecting the POWs in other ways, leaving them alone to wither and die in their cold cells. In fact, as the war intensified, so did the pressure to provide material for the North Vietnamese propaganda campaign. Delegations from Iron Curtain countries, as well as some sympathetic westerners, were escorted through the country to inspect bomb damage, talk to wounded civilians, and, more and more, meet with American POWs. Plantation was the most presentable camp. It had been a colonial estate at one time, and while it had lost whatever grandeur it had once had and grown shabby under the demands of its military mission, compared to Hoa Lo or some of the other camps it looked almost benign. So most of the delegations were brought there, as were the POWs who seemed likely to make a good impression on the visiting foreigners.

What the Vietnamese wanted from the prisoners who met with delegations was simple enough: they wanted them to say that they were being treated well and without brutality. This was especially true after the Stratton bowing episode, which had turned out badly for the Vietnamese. Stratton's performance had set off a flurry of charges and speculation about brainwashing and torture. The North Vietnamese were widely condemned for mistreating prisoners. They were embarrassed and lost face. While they could not suddenly allow the International Red Cross to inspect the camps — the truth would have been a more severe embarrassment and propaganda setback — they did bring in sympathetic delegations to meet with more cooperative POWs.

They made sure that the men who met the delegations

would be cooperative. Before a man met with a delegation, he would be taken out of his cell, up to the Big House, and "asked" if he would like to meet with some visitors to North Vietnam.

A few men would agree immediately and eagerly. They were in Plantation because they were not resisters and, in some cases, were just short of being active collaborators. They had been broken to the point where they wanted above all else to please and accommodate their captors.

But other prisoners in Plantation would belligerently refuse to cooperate and take whatever they had coming. One of these was Bud Day, an air force pilot who later received the Medal of Honor for his conduct as a POW. When asked if he would agree to meet with a delegation, Day would answer, "No. Not now. Not ever."

He would be beaten, put in the ropes, thrown in solitary. Eventually, the Vietnamese thought, he would break and would meet with the delegation; or they might just give up. But the next time he was asked, Day would give the same answer, and the ritual would begin once more. For the seven years that he was a prisoner in North Vietnam, Day maintained a posture of unyielding antagonism and contempt for his captors. Whenever they asked if he would like to meet with a delegation, he would answer, "No. Not now. Not ever."

Most of the men in Plantation fell somewhere between these extremes. They were not willing to meet with a delegation simply to please their captors, but they were not able to resist, over and over, to the point of undergoing torture. It was not a matter, merely, of preference. A man who had been tortured would not always stop at his first line of defense. Once he broke, he broke completely, and then he would give not just what he had to give, or could get by with giving, but anything that he thought the interrogators might want or that could, in some way, help him. It was always better if he was not broken. Better for him and his comrades. Because when a man was broken, he would routinely betray them and make things worse for everyone in the camp. Better, where possible, to avoid being tortured and broken.

Which was easily said but harder in practice. The men didn't want to make it easy for the enemy or unnecessarily hard for themselves. They had to find a way to maneuver inside a vague sort of no man's land where notions of duty, pride, self-esteem, and survival shifted in and out of focus and the support of their comrades became the one fixed and reliable landmark by which they could navigate.

It was Stratton's job to provide leadership and guidance as the senior ranking officer in Plantation. (From time to time there were men in Plantation who were senior to him, but they were held in isolated cells and could not exercise command effectively, so they would delegate authority to Stratton.) According to the Code of Conduct, it was his duty to assume command — to make rules and set policy where possible and to maintain some semblance of unity and camp morale. It was a demanding, thankless job, one for which there was no possible preparation. Stratton fell back on his common sense, his Jesuit education, and the lessons of his own experience.

He knew, first, that every man had his limit. He had been tortured to his limit to make the tape that was played for the delegation before he appeared to be photographed bowing like an automaton. At one point, during the worst of it, he did not have to be put in the ropes before he would say what the interrogators wanted him to say. The threat of the ropes alone was enough.

So he knew that a man who had been truly broken would not merely cooperate in a minimal, defensive fashion but would do whatever it took — whatever he *thought* it would take — to stop the torture and make his tormentors leave him alone. A man who had been broken would actually volunteer information that the interrogators had not even asked for. He would do, or say, virtually anything.

So, logically, the objective was to avoid being broken; to avoid those situations where you might be broken and then compromise yourself and, perhaps, your comrades. The Vietnamese might torture a man for refusing to meet with a delegation, or to find out what kind of radar his plane carried, but once he started talking, especially if he was beyond the limit of his endurance, he might volunteer information about the camp's chain of command, or secret communications, or something else of value to the POWs in the camp. He could not help himself. The consequences would be bad for the other men in the camp and disastrous for the man's own pride, making him that much more vulnerable next time around.

The point, then, was to avoid being put in a position of being tortured and broken over something pointless.

But unyielding cooperation with the Vietnamese was not a solution. First, because the POW's own sense of duty would not allow it and, then, because cooperation would not be enough. The Vietnamese would simply raise the stakes. Men would be pressured to collaborate, to make sweeping propaganda statements, to do whatever their captors thought necessary. It was important — crucial — to resist.

For Al Stafford, as for any other POW, unified, disciplined resistance was a big step on the way back up from the very bottom which he had touched during those four humiliating days in the Green Knobby Room at Hoa Lo. He had been broken, in despair, on the verge of suicide or insanity. Then he had experienced something like a rebirth, revived by the simple satisfactions of companionship and the knowledge that he had not been the only one to break. In the cell with Parrott and Sawhill he had still been an impotent captive, but at least he was not isolated and alone in his disgrace.

Now, in the room with Stratton where he was in communication with the entire camp, he was joining an active resistance. In some way he was fighting back, which made the hunger, the cold, and the uncertainty if not bearable then at least something he could put to one side while he concentrated on more important things — little things that achieved the large result of letting him lose himself in the cause.

Active resistance, however, was a relative term under these circumstances. Escape, of course, was the highest form of resistance and was listed in the Code of Conduct as one of the POW's explicit duties. But escape was virtually impossible, doomed in the absence of outside help from sympathetic Vietnamese. There was simply no way a Caucasian could move through the densely populated area around Hanoi without being spotted, and a failed attempt would result in extra pressure on the men who were not involved. The risk was not worth any possible benefits.

So resistance took less spectacular forms, and success was measured less by concrete accomplishments than by a psychological sense of not giving in, of doing *something*, however trivial, to frustrate the North Vietnamese.

Among the POWs there were two schools of thought regarding resistance. One favored a harder, more inflexible and confrontational posture. If the guards wanted you to stand when they came into your cell, then you remained seated and made them force you to stand, even if it meant you took a beating.

The other, softer school held that you simply wasted reserves by fighting battles that you could not win, and that having lost them, you left yourself weaker for the next fight, which might be more important. The objective was to stay strong and unified, to maneuver, and to pick your battles. Since anyone could be broken, provocation was pointless.

Stratton was identified with the softer school, chiefly because of the bowing incident. Like most aviators who had seen the pictures of Stratton in *Life,* Al Stafford admired him for making a brave, resourceful, and effective gesture. Anyone who saw those pictures, he thought, would immediately understand the truth behind them. But some of the POWs in the camps had not seen the pictures; they had only heard Stratton's taped confession, played over the camp loudspeaker, and they believed he had given in too easily.

The disagreement threatened to divide the POWs when they most needed to be unified. But in Plantation, where the men knew Stratton by his orders and his example, they accepted his decisions and leadership and developed an intense loyalty to him. They respected him for the theory of resistance that evolved under his command. As it turned out, his ideas also became policy in other camps, under the direction of other senior officers. Expediency under extreme conditions had led to essentially the same conclusions.

The fundamental rule was that POWs were still bound to resist. Willing, uncoerced collaboration was out of the question. No man, however, was expected to force a confrontation. In fact, under Stratton's leadership "head buttings" were discouraged. He understood the value the Vietnamese place on "face" and passed instructions through the wall that advised against putting the guards and interrogators in a position where they would lose face and be forced to retaliate. To do so was to risk being tortured and broken, in which case a man might give up more than he had to, for no good purpose.

There were concessions the Vietnamese wanted that were

not worth fighting over. If they wanted POWs to stand when a guard entered their cell, then it was not worth a head butting to refuse. You stood when a guard entered the room. You might take your time, get to your feet like an old, brittle man; but you did not go to war over the issue.

In some cases it was possible to cooperate and resist simultaneously. For instance, the Vietnamese demanded that POWs read the news over the camp radio. This "news" was a scripted, politicized version of events. Even when they had no news of the outside world from recent shootdowns, the POWs recognized that the information put together by the Vietnamese was preposterous. But it had to be read over the camp loudspeaker by a POW. Under Stratton's guidance the men at Plantation agreed to read the news rather than resist and go into the ropes. But when they read, it was in the halting fashion of second graders, stumbling over words and pronunciations, ignoring punctuation, and stressing the wrong syllables, so that when the Americans were said to be "putting up obstacles to peace," the word came out "ob-STACK-els." Some men were considered especially good at reading the camp news; one was admired for the way he described the defeat of a battalion of American marines in a battle fought near the "demoralized zone." Guards could not understand why so many of the prisoners seemed to think the camp news was funny, but to punish them for laughing would be to lose face. So the POWs won a small victory there.

It was even possible to give in and resist simultaneously when the Vietnamese wanted a man to meet with a delegation. This was always an ordeal, but there were times when the alternative was a head butting and then the ropes. You did what you had to do, and sometimes you came out ahead.

Stafford was an unlikely choice for such a meeting. He had lost a lot of weight owing to the diet of soup, and he still suffered from intestinal parasites. His broken arm had shrunk and withered without treatment. Still, he was taken from the cell one day, marched up to the Big House, and asked if he would like to meet with a visiting delegation.

He answered carefully, wanting above all to avoid a head butting and more torture.

"I'd better not," he said, trying to sound accommodating.

"Why, Stafford?"

"Well, because I have worms and no medicine to get rid of them. The worms give me dysentery, and I cannot always control myself. It would be embarrassing if I lost control in front of a delegation."

The Vietnamese, who are culturally modest about sex and bodily functions, did not force the issue, and Stafford was returned to his cell.

But it was never that easy. A few days later they returned, and this time they did not ask. In the Big House he was told to sit on a small, three-legged stool. He waited for several minutes, alone in the room. Then an interrogator arrived and told him that he had been selected to meet with a delegation of visitors from Eastern Bloc countries.

Stafford tried the line about the worms and his dysentery.

The interrogator shook his head. "You will meet with the delegation, or you will be punished."

Stafford refused and felt his stomach lurch. For a moment he thought he might actually lose control, right there on the stool.

"You must meet with the delegation, or you will be punished," the interrogator said. By now, Stafford and the other POWs had learned to distinguish between threats that were serious and those that were idle and could be disregarded, at least temporarily. This interrogator was serious.

Stafford said nothing. He was in a head butting, and anything he said would only make it worse.

The interrogator left the room, and Stafford waited with

rising apprehension for him to return with other men, carrying the ropes.

But they did not use the ropes this time. Instead, Stafford was forced to remain sitting until he reconsidered. At first he felt a vast sense of relief. Compared to the ropes, this would be easy.

The hours passed. First his back and his arms began to ache. Then his whole body. He was not allowed to sleep. If he nodded off, still sitting on the stool, the guards would prod him in his tender, healing ribs to wake him up. He began to crave sleep, to stare at the floor and imagine himself lying there for just ten minutes.

Worse than being denied sleep, though, was going without water. Since his ordeal in the Green Knobby Room, when he'd not had water for four or five days — he would never know exactly how long it had been — Stafford had felt a horror of the notion of prolonged thirst. He remembered crawling on the floor and licking the walls for any moisture that had seeped through the stone. In his mind that had been the essence of degradation. He knew that he would do anything before he went through that again. When it was over he had gulped untreated water from a cistern and still suffered from worms as a result. Bad as the worms were, he would do it again if he were ever that thirsty.

Finally, after two days, he gave in. It was not worth being broken again.

"I will meet your delegation," he told the Vietnamese.

"Good, Stafford," they said. "You have a good attitude."

He was kept in a small holding cell in the Big House, probably so that he would not be contaminated by the presence of other Americans and encouraged to change his mind. After he had been given some water and allowed to sleep, the interrogators began briefing him on what to say to the delegation.

"You will tell them you have been given the lenient and

humane treatment by the people of the Democratic Republic of Vietnam."

Stafford nodded.

"Say it."

"I have been given the lenient and humane treatment by the people of the Democratic Republic of Vietnam," Stafford said mechanically.

"Good, Stafford. You have a good attitude."

Stafford lay awake under his mosquito net that night, agonizing over his decision. Had he really needed a drink of water and a few minutes' sleep *that* badly? How would he feel in the morning, when he had to perform for the tame East German and Polish journalists who were here for some canned quotes about how well the Vietnamese were treating their captives? How would he feel when he went back to Warehouse One and told Stratton, Chauncey, and Sawhill about meeting the delegation? How long would it be before the Vietnamese came to him again, telling him he had to meet with another delegation? Better, in a way, Stafford thought, if they had hauled out the ropes. When they bent you, then it was okay to break. There was no ambiguity then.

In the morning Stafford was briefed again.

"Now, Stafford, when you are asked, you will say that you have received the lenient and humane treatment from the people of the Democratic Republic of Vietnam."

Once more he nodded.

"Say it."

"I have received the lenient and humane treatment from the people of the Democratic Republic of Vietnam."

"Good."

He was taken to a large room in a building behind the Big House. It was the room where the guards watched movies, and it had been furnished today with a long table facing several rows of chairs. There were floodlights aimed at the table, where Stafford was told to sit. He looked out into the room at the stolid, unrecognizable faces and experienced the indignity of being studied. To these people he was merely a specimen. He hated it, and he hated them.

He was asked to give his name and the usual background data. He recited it in the deadest, most vacant tone he could manage. Be damned if he would let any of the potato faces out there think he was doing this willingly.

"Commander Stafford," one of the journalists said haughtily, "would you tell us how you have been treated since you were captured."

Stafford saw an opening of sorts. It wasn't much, just a crease, but then in his situation you took what you could get.

"Since I was captured I have received the lenient and humane treatment from the people of the Democratic Republic of Vietnam."

The interrogators, standing to either side of him, seemed pleased. He had given exactly the right answer. But Stafford also felt some fractional sense of triumph. Nobody in the world who could still recognize truth when he saw it would believe that an American aviator would talk that way unless it were under duress. *The* lenient and humane treatment? That small article, a three-letter word, invalidated the whole dog and pony show. He may not have won the round, but he hadn't lost it either.

When he was returned to Warehouse One, he told his roommates about his strategy and they congratulated him. "Good job," Stratton said.

"Yeah," Chauncey agreed. "That was shit-hot, Al."

The struggle in Plantation and the other camps turned on such small victories in this obscure battle.

But the larger question remained unresolved, looming over every decision the POWs made and every action they took when dealing with the Vietnamese. Should they resist? Yes, obviously and unquestionably. But how far? How much should a man expect from himself and his comrades? What was the limit? How much was enough? Every man in Plantation hungered for an answer to that question as much as he craved a good meal.

Well, Stratton said at first, resist as long as you can. This was refined later to "as long as is prudent." And finally, "to the point of serious or permanent injury." It was always a subjective evaluation, but the rule was: Don't make it too easy for them or too hard on yourself.

As important as it was to hold out and make it hard for the enemy, it was equally vital — perhaps even more so — for a man to regather his strength after he had been broken, to pull himself together, put his defeat behind him, and get back on the team. When he returned from an interrogation and torture, it was crucial that he tell his fellow POWs what he had said. He could not hide anything from them, try to work both sides of the street. That was implicit in the code. A man must "keep faith with his fellow prisoners."

The essential point was not to give up completely once you had been broken but to rally. Jeremiah Denton, in another camp, had come to essentially the same policy conclusion and given it a name that stuck — Bouncing Back.

The formulation of the Bounce Back policy was the conceptual and spiritual answer that the POWs had been looking for, and they clung to it like a life raft, in spite of the fact that it was in many ways alien to the military way of thinking, which does not recognize subtle or shifting distinctions. The military academies subscribe to an honor system that does not allow for shadings of right and wrong, and the Code of Conduct did not take into account individual thresholds of pain. But life in Plantation and the other camps imposed its own reality, and the men had to make new rules and learn to live by them. Bouncing back was the logical, inevitable standard, and it was, in its way, demanding and unforgiving. It required a man to make an honest assessment of his own toughness, which was hard enough; but it also required him to take on faith another man's assessment of *his* ability to endure torture, and this was even more difficult. The temptation was always to believe that you should have held out longer and, thus, get down on yourself, or, worse, to think that another man should have done better and get down on him. Before the Bounce Back doctrine could work, the POWs had to believe in themselves and one another. It required a large measure of faith and trust. The alternative was a disintegration of unity and morale. Bounce Back worked for a number of reasons: because Stratton and other senior officers provided firm leadership; because the men were trained to obey their lawful superiors (in this regard the Code of Conduct was invaluable); and because the alternatives were either impossible or unthinkable. It was either Bounce Back or every man for himself.

■═■═■

Seven

NOT EVERYBODY IN Plantation was willing to obey
Stratton's orders or to live by the Bounce Back doctrine. Most were, and they would later say that Stratton's leadership and the amended Code of Conduct enabled
them to survive and to leave Vietnam with a sense of having
done their duty. But there were exceptions, which the Vietnamese were quick to exploit.

Prisoners who cooperated willingly, who did not bother
with even a pretense of resistance, were separated from the
others in Plantation. Instead of being placed in one of the
cells in the long warehouse, where they would share a common wall with those who were resisting and obeying Stratton's orders as they were tapped, laboriously, from cell to
cell, these men lived in a cell next to the room where Stafford had met the delegation and stated that he was receiving
the lenient and humane treatment. The men in this cell were
not reachable by the tap code. They could communicate only
with one another.

It was plain to the other men in the camp that the Vietnamese had something in mind for these men. At first the
other prisoners assumed that it was merely making tapes
and films, meeting with delegations, and other useful propaganda stunts. These men were given extra rations and more

variety in their food. They received medical attention and were even allowed out of their cell. The other prisoners resented the special treatment given to the "tame guys" and the obvious nonchalance with which they accepted it. Still, they believed that somehow those men could be turned around; that if they could be reached, they would get back on the team.

But it became apparent, sometime in January 1968, that the Vietnamese had truly special plans for these men. They were being fitted for clothes to replace their prison pajamas. They were taken out of the prison from time to time for sightseeing tours, during which they would inspect bomb damage and meet with wounded Vietnamese. They were indoctrinated, repeatedly, in the North Vietnamese line about the war — its causes and prospects for its end. Eventually the men were told the reason for this extra attention, and the word quickly spread around the camp. They were going to be sent home.

This was insupportable to the other POWs. While it had been necessary to revise the code on the matter of how much a man would be required to suffer before he went beyond name, rank, serial number, and date of birth, there was no compelling reason to modify its language or intent where special favors and parole were concerned. There was simply no excuse for accepting either.

Stratton was desperate for some form of communication with these men. He wanted to send them clear and unambiguous orders not to accept parole. Stratton realized that, even if he could get to these men, they might not obey his orders. But he had decided, characteristically, to make the best of a bad situation. If they did refuse to obey his orders and did accept early release, then at least they could be persuaded to memorize some names and get the information back to the States. This became something of an obsession with the POWs. If the people at home knew names, then someday they could demand an accounting. A man whose name was known, who had been identified conclusively as a captive of the North Vietnamese, would not be allowed simply to disappear. To the POWs this was an article of faith.

One day Stratton and Al Stafford were let out of Warehouse One, under guard, and taken to the end of the courtyard for their routine bath, shave, and opportunity to handwash their clothes. It was a break, of sorts, merely to get out of the cell and walk through the courtyard, under the bare branches of the tall trees. But on this day even that small pleasure was diminished by the tension that had been created in the camp, and in the minds of the resisters, by the prospects of the early release.

The washroom was merely a small shed at the end of the camp, made of brick and mortar. It was one of those places that never quite dry out, so mold and fungus grew abundantly in the joints between the walls and floors. Insects and lizards thrived in this environment.

The bathhouse had been divided into four stalls with a large cistern in each. On the floor of each stall there was a small hole covered by an iron trap. The hole led to a drainpipe that was common to all four stalls, and the POWs had quickly discovered that they could remove the traps and talk through the drainpipe to the man in the next stall. The Vietnamese would never come into the stalls when the men were naked and bathing, and the pipe seemed to contain noise so that conversation could not be heard outside. If you kept your voice down, you could pass information to a man from another cell or another part of the camp who might have been taken out for his bath at the same time, a man you knew only as an abbreviated name tapped through the wall.

Stratton stepped into one of the middle stalls. He knew

that Stafford was in the next stall, so when he heard the sounds of a man in the other adjacent cell, he got down on his hands and knees, removed the trap, and spoke softly into the drainpipe, first asking who was there. The man in the next cell answered, after a few hesitant moments, and the name jolted Stratton like a shock of electricity. It was one of the three men about to be released.

Stratton took a moment to calm himself, knowing that if he came on too hard and tough, the man might simply refuse to talk. He took a long breath, let it out, and then began to speak in a mild, almost conversational voice. But he didn't have much time, so he got right to the point.

"All right," he said. "I know who you are. Now, do you know who I am?"

Yes, the man said, he knew who Stratton was.

"Okay, then you also know that I am the SRO in this camp."

The man said that he knew this, too.

"And that any orders I issue should be considered as coming from competent authority." Stratton hoped the military locutions would have an effect.

"Yes," the man said in a noncommittal tone.

"All right, then, I am giving you a direct, lawful order — right now — not to accept parole from the enemy. Do you understand?"

Stafford was also on his hands and knees, listening through the drain in his stall. The pause that followed Stratton's question seemed to freeze time in its tracks. Finally, the answer came, weak yet firm at the same time.

"Sorry, but I'm going home."

Stafford wanted to scream through the pipe, but he stopped himself. It was Stratton's play, and his next words were characteristically calm and rational, even through the distortions of the pipe.

"All right," Stratton said, "that's your decision. But if you choose to disobey my order and accept early release, then at least do something for your fellow prisoners when you go. Try to memorize some of the names on the list."

This time the voice came back with more confidence. "No," the man said, "I've never been any good at memorizing, and I've got too much on my mind anyway. All I can think about is home."

Stafford could not remember ever feeling such desperate, murderous frustration. He wanted to crawl through the drainpipe and get his hands on the man. Stratton was saying something, in a louder, angry voice, but the man would not answer. He was through talking and he was going home. The guard shouted for Stafford and Stratton to hurry up. With his fingers trembling, Stafford replaced the iron trap, dried off, and stepped out into the yard. Stratton stood next to him, his face as pale as wax and his dark eyes burning. They walked to Warehouse One, feeling more than ever the rage of helplessness, the impotence of the captive.

They told Sawhill and Chauncey about what had happened, and for a few moments they enjoyed the false sense of release that comes from raging against your enemies. Then, when they had finished with the name calling, they got on the wall and passed the information along to the rest of the men in the camp. The sound of the tapping seemed especially hollow and dispirited, and that night they did not talk.

A day or two later the three prisoners were handed over to the custody of the antiwar activists Daniel Berrigan and Howard Zinn. They represented one of many ad hoc groups in the United States that were opposed to the war and believed that some independent channel of communication with the North Vietnamese might bring it to an end. Some of these groups believed that the North Vietnamese had no aggressive intentions, while other, more extreme groups desired not a negotiated settlement of the war but a North Vietnamese victory. They accepted North Vietnamese claims about the treatment of prisoners either on faith or after reassurances from North Vietnamese officials and staged interviews with carefully selected POWs. The other POWs, some of whom were tortured into meeting with these delegations, despised them all. But unless one of their own men, a resister, somehow made it out in one of the orchestrated releases, there was no way of getting out their message. While most of the POWs considered themselves stalemated and locked out of this game being played between the North Vietnamese and the antiwar groups, Stratton was coming up with a plan. For the moment, however, he kept it to himself. He had other, more immediate problems to deal with: chiefly, the matter of deteriorating morale.

When the three early releases had gone, the Vietnamese broadcast over the camp radio their confessions of war crimes, apologies to the Vietnamese people, and prayers that they would not be sent back to bomb the country again (which was not simply unlikely but close to impossible). To the men in Plantation, shivering under their thin blankets in the weak light of bare bulbs that burned night and day in their bleak cells, listening to those tapes was, in some way, like being shot down and captured all over again. When they got on the wall, they raged against the "slimies" who had taken early release and swore retribution when they got home — in the form of a court-martial, at least, and something more personal if that didn't work out. In their own minds, however, they were convinced that those three men had made a profound personal mistake. Even so, it was hard not to think of home and to see their own attempts at resistance as small and useless.

*

This episode was, in a way, the most demanding test of Bounce Back. In this case it was not simply a question of one man rebounding from torture and the subsequent feelings of humiliation over having cooperated. Here the entire camp had been disgraced. Now they could either fall into apathy and acquiescence or pull themselves together and begin to resist again. Stratton, who had been the most publicly humiliated of all the POWs by his bowing performance, was, paradoxically, the ideal man to lead Plantation out of the gloom and demoralization that followed the defeat represented by the early releases. The entire camp had to shake this one off and get back to resisting, and it was his duty to set the example and lead the way from his pitiful command post in Warehouse One.

His genius as a POW and camp SRO was his ability to rally in body and spirit and to use his supple mind to find opportunity in what looked like a hopeless situation, as he had when he was struck with the inspiration to bow like a man who had been drugged or brainwashed. He had a gift for making chicken salad out of chicken shit, the other POWs said admiringly. In strict military parlance, it was called resourcefulness.

So he began formulating orders and policies and simple inspirational messages to send out through the wall. These messages were tapped almost constantly over the next several weeks. Remember that you are United States military officers, he told the other prisoners. It is your duty to resist, to obey the lawful orders of your superior officers, and to conduct yourselves according to the highest standards . . .

It sounded absurd under the circumstances, but with repetition, the message struck nerves up and down the cells. We lost that one, Stratton told his men, and we might lose some more. But we can't quit.

New men were moved into the isolated cell next to the

theater, and plans were obviously under way for more releases. Stratton and the other men in Warehouse One began
writing a long message, using toilet paper, ink made from
brick dust, and for a pen, a bamboo sliver sharpened on the
rough concrete floor.

The long message took the form of a military order. It
was written in the official language and format and ad-
dressed the question of early release specifically, and the
duties of an American prisoner of war in general. The plan
was to smuggle this "official" document into the cell where
the men being groomed for early release were being held.
Stratton wanted to get to them early, before they had been
fully compromised and felt that they had no choice but to
go through with whatever deal they had made.

It was an obvious tactic. The early releases were kept in
isolation precisely in order to keep them from hearing the
arguments of the other POWs, especially the senior men,
who could speak with the kind of authority to which military
habit would grant respect. The problem became how to get
the elaborate orders to the isolation cell so that they might
have some effect.

The solution was to find a courier. Some men were taken
out of their cells every day to perform camp housekeeping
duties. They would collect, dump, and rinse out waste buckets. They would go to the kitchen to pick up the vat of
pumpkin soup, then take it from cell to cell so the prisoners
could fill their bowls. They were sent to work in an area
behind the kitchen, mixing coal dust and water, then shap-
ing the paste into small briquets called coal balls which, when
dried, would be used for cooking. A man on one of these
details might get a chance, when the guards were distracted,
to throw the message through the bars of the cell where the
candidates for early release were being held.

It was a long shot, and it involved considerable risk. Any

man who volunteered to serve as a courier was also volunteering for the ropes if he were caught. Torture was certain enough, for reasons that were arbitrary, and the risk might not seem worth the benefit. What, after all, was in it for the courier? He was hanging it out to save the pride of the slimies. It was even possible that one of the men being held for early release would report a successful delivery in order to curry favor. There were instructions telling the isolated men how to get a message back to Stratton, through a secret mail drop. The early release candidates might decide to give its location away. Communications would be compromised, and the men who were resisting would suffer. The objective was unity, but that was a vague goal against the hard memory of the ropes.

Still, all four men in Warehouse One were willing to try. The first question was how to conceal the little bundle of paper. A man could not carry it in his hand or anywhere else on his body where the Vietnamese might spot a bulge in his prison pajamas and subject him to a search.

The answer was to tie the papers to the courier's genitals.

"They aren't likely to search you there," Stratton said, "even if they do suspect something."

So every time one of the men from Warehouse One left the cell for camp details, he carried the order tied with string to his private parts. He watched the cell where the early releases were being held and waited for his chance. Most days it did not come, and he would return to the cell, still carrying the papers.

"Sonofabitch but this thing gets *heavy*," Stafford would say when he came back to the cell.

"Yeah, but look at it as exercise. Just think what it does for your physique," a cellmate would reply.

Finally Stafford saw his chance, on the way to the mess hall to spend the morning making coal balls. The normal lethargy of the camp seemed a little more pronounced than usual. His guard dropped several steps behind him and then stopped to talk to another guard and smoke a cigarette. For the moment, he was paying no attention to the American wearing droopy pajamas who shuffled along dispiritedly ahead of him. Stafford simply kept walking, as though he had not noticed that he was unescorted. He moved like a man numbed by circumstances, but his mind was racing, approaching overload the way it did just before roll in on a mission. He tried to shut everything out, to focus his attention on the cell where the early releases were being held, just a few more steps ahead of him. He took a quick, furtive look over his shoulder, saw that his guard was still smoking and talking, and reached inside his pajamas and untied the string. His mouth was dry and his legs were weak as he stepped a few paces off his normal route, so that he passed within a couple of feet of the cell. He tried to walk with the normal shuffling gait of a POW, to move with no haste or urgency, though everything inside of him wanted to rush to the cell and with one sudden gesture be rid of the incriminating package and all the risk that it contained. He made himself move like a shoplifter browsing the aisles.

When he was next to the cell window, he raised his good arm high enough to reach the sill and, like a basketball player tapping in a rebound, flicked his wrist and let the package fall from his hand. He listened for angry shouts and tensed for the impact of a fist or a rifle butt aimed from behind. But nobody said anything. Nobody raised a hand against him.

For the next four hours he made coal balls with trembling fingers. He could not keep his eyes or his mind on the job, expecting the arrival of guards any minute, come to take him up to the Big House, where he would be "severely punished" for violating camp rules. If they tortured him, he would say that the message had been his idea and that he had written it himself and signed Stratton's name. He wondered if he would be able to stick to that line even if they made him go without water. Whenever the guard moved, or spoke to another Vietnamese in the yard, Stafford's stomach twisted into a tight knot. Even when the work was done, he did not relax until he had been led back across the yard and returned to Warehouse One.

When the door was closed and locked behind him, he broke into a smile, gave a thumbs up, and said, "Mission accomplished."

The other men in the cell smiled back and pounded him on his shoulders and back, being careful to stay away from the injured spots. "Goddamn, Al, baby. Way to go, man. Shit-hot job."

It was like coming back to the carrier after a tough hop, flown well, and catching the three wire. And, as with any mission, the long-term results seemed unimportant and trivial. It might be a pointless skirmish in a bad war, absolutely meaningless against the big picture, but he had, by God, done his job. He knew it, and his comrades knew it. The rest was just so much bullshit.

Typical of the war in Vietnam, Stafford's successful mission yielded small and ambiguous results. Some of the men who read the order were persuaded to turn down early release. But the Vietnamese found replacements for them. The antiwar delegations were still eager to accept prisoners for return to the United States, and the Vietnamese continued to groom men who seemed to be good prospects and to release them to the custody of sympathetic Americans. So the mission did not accomplish its largest, most ambitious objective. But by succeeding, Stafford had "rescued" one or two men who were vacillating, and, more important, he had *done* something. The news went out over the wall in a crisply tapped message, and the return messages were full of congratulations and "Well dones," which Stafford valued more than the decoration he received after the war was over for his actions. Getting that message through to the isolated cell had helped to stiffen the resolve and raise the spirits of the other men in Plantation. It allowed them to feel that they were still resisting, and that the war, no matter how hopeless it looked, was still going on.

Eight

ON MARCH 31, 1968, President Lyndon Johnson spoke to the American people and announced that he was suspending bombing of North Vietnam above the twentieth parallel. At the conclusion of the speech, he announced that he would not be running for reelection. He had been defeated by the North Vietnamese; he was quitting and going home. It remained to be seen if the POWs would be so lucky.

They learned of Johnson's decision through the camp news and from information brought in by new shootdowns. They did not need anyone to tell them that the bombing had been stopped, and when there was nothing said about their release, many of them drew the most severe conclusion. Stratton said to the other men in the room, "If we weren't part of some deal — no more bombing in exchange for our release — then we are going to be here for a long time. Probably until they start bombing again." Most of the other men in Plantation found this analysis insupportably pessimistic, so they watched for hopeful signs. Any change of routine, a new line of questioning in interrogation, the appearance of a new guard or interrogator, the arrival of a truck or jeep in the camp — each of these things was studied like some kind of portent full of meaning. Countless tapped messages began with the words "What is the significance of . . . ?"

On a day in April, when the weather had warmed enough
that it was no longer necessary to spend the day wrapped in
a blanket, shivering, the food detail appeared as usual at the
door of Warehouse One, but instead of thin soup the prisoners were given small fried bananas and some boiled greens.

The change was too momentous for study or interpreta-
tion. The men simply ate.

"Goddamn, Arv," Stafford said to Chauncey, "this tastes
like fried country ham and collard greens."

"I don't know, Al," Chauncey answered between bites. "I
think it tastes even better than that."

"As good as a T-bone with a baked potato on the side and
a Caesar salad?"

"Close."

"How about a plate of fried chicken with rice and gravy
and homemade biscuits?"

"Just about that good, I'd say. Maybe a little better."

When they finished, Stafford said, "What do you suppose
it *means*? We haven't been fed anything like that as long as
I've been here. It's got to mean something."

"I don't know what's behind it, Al, but you know something?"

"What's that?"

"Whatever it is, I'm for it."

The walls were alive with messages about the change in rations, most of them beginning with the inevitable phrase,
"What is the significance of . . . ?" The answer, it turned
out, was "Not much."

Hanoi was no longer being bombed, but the air war went
on in the Panhandle of North Vietnam, and new shootdowns arrived with the unwelcome news that the war was
still going on. No negotiations yet, and no reason to believe
that peace and repatriation were at hand.

A single rail line ran outside of Plantation, just beyond

the back wall of the warehouse, and the men in Stafford's cell could lean a sleeping pallet against the wall, climb the ladderlike studs that held the boards together, and look through the gun ports at the passing trains. Even after Johnson's decision to halt the bombing of Hanoi, the passing cattle cars were full of young men in uniform on their way to the fight. More vividly than any news from recent shootdowns, or the small seeds of truth planted in the propaganda of the camp news, this was proof that the war was not winding down.

Guards still came to take prisoners up to the Big House for interrogations, but, increasingly, these became what the POWs called "temperature quizzes." Instead of being pumped for military information or pressed for propaganda, the men were asked how they were getting along and how they felt about their captors and the war. Most of the POWs maneuvered to avoid head buttings. They answered vaguely and, eventually, were returned to their cells. They began to suspect that, in many cases, the quizzes were merely a pretext used by interrogators who wanted to practice their English. Still, to see the door open and the guard point his finger at you was a frightening experience. There was no way of knowing, when you left the cell for the walk up to the Big House, if you were in for a temperature quiz or something else, something a lot more serious. Delegations were still coming into Vietnam for tours; prisoners at all the camps were still being pressured to make statements and, at Plantation, accept early release; punishments were still being inflicted on men who were caught violating camp rules, especially those forbidding communication between prisoners.

The weeks and months that followed Tet, then, were not better by any objective measure.

So the POWs began psychologically digging in, adjusting for the long haul. Most were in their twenties or early thirties.

A few were barely old enough to have voted in one election before they were shot down. Some were fathers of children they'd never seen, husbands of women they had lived with for only a few weeks. It seemed increasingly possible — probable, even — that they would be middle aged or older before they left Vietnam. Their survival now included facing, somehow, this hard reality. They had to find ways to fill those years, to salvage something from their youth.

They began by trying to make the best of the physical conditions of their captivity. They would never be comfortable — the cells were crowded and unventilated, and the men slept on boards and wore the same clothes day after day — but they could try to keep clean, and they could improvise ways to reduce their misery.

In Warehouse Four there was a prisoner named Tom Hall who was an especially gifted improviser. Among his fellow prisoners he was known as a man who could "make do."

Hall was a farm boy from outside Suffolk, Virginia, who had grown up learning how to doctor animals, fix cars, and make all of the endless repairs necessary to keep a farm running. He had graduated from Virginia Tech, gone into the navy, and learned to fly fighters. He had been stationed on the *Bon Homme Richard,* on Yankee Station, when his F-8 was hit by a SAM. He went to afterburner and pointed the plane toward the beach. When he was over the Gulf of Tonkin, safely out of reach of the patrol boats and fishing junks that sometimes captured pilots who bailed out over water, he ejected from his burning plane. The rescue helicopter picked him up and flew him back to the carrier, where the captain of the ship was waiting on the flight deck to greet him. A photographer caught the moment — Hall and the captain smiling and shaking hands, Hall still wearing his drenched flight suit. The picture made the papers back in the United States.

Like any pilot who had ejected, Hall was ordered to stand

down for a day. The following morning the weather was so bad over North Vietnam that no missions were flown from the ship. But the next day Hall was flying again. He caught another SAM, and this time he bailed out near Hanoi. He had been shot down twice in four days. That was June 1967.

To the men who shared space with him in North Vietnam, Tom Hall was the perfect roommate. He knew how to be quiet, and when he talked, he always had something interesting to say. He told stories about life on the farm, including one about how his family kept a hummingbird in the house, flying free, to keep the bugs down. The other pilots loved this story; the idea of a hummingbird in the house was somehow otherworldly.

Everyone liked Tom Hall. He never got too high or too low. He maintained an even strain, as pilots say, and he looked after his comrades first and himself second. He didn't bitch and he didn't quit and he knew, by God, how to cope.

It was Hall who figured out how to handle the problem of the cold in the drafty cells at Plantation in the winter of 1968, when the men would wake up in the morning close to hypothermia and spend the first hour or two of the day trying to warm up.

HATS, he tapped through the wall. Use extra cloth, or better a sock, to make a hat. Stretch it out until it will fit over your head like a watch cap. You lose most of your body heat through your head, he explained, and this would help. The men tried it, and it worked.

Still, it was cold, especially at night.

MOSQUITO NETS, Hall tapped. When it is below forty outside, he explained, mosquitoes are the least of your problems. You do not need to sleep under a net. But the net can be turned into a kind of insulation, he went on, like the fishnet stuff that Scandinavians use for underwear. Before you lie down to go to sleep, wrap your upper body in your mosquito net.

The improvised underwear also worked. The men were not exactly warm, but they weren't cold to the bone any longer.

Tom Hall also improvised sewing needles out of fish bones scrounged from the mess halls, or from pieces of wire picked up in the yard, and these made it possible for the POWs to mend their clothes. They even learned to amuse themselves by doing a kind of needlepoint. The favorite pattern was, far and away, the American flag.

Hall was also given credit for discovering that a man could use his sandals, which were cut from old rubber tires, as a kind of toilet seat by laying them across the cold, sharp, dirty edges of the bucket before he squatted. This, in the minds of many POWs, was the most inspired piece of improvisation in the entire war.

Another persistent, seemingly insoluble problem at Plantation was the rats. They were abundant and they were bold. It was possible to chase them out of the cell during the day, but they returned at night and moved around at will. Men were frequently awakened by the pressure of small feet moving across their chests.

Using items that he scrounged, pieces of metal, string, and an empty tin can, Hall built a working mousetrap. So his cell, at least, was spared a rat infestation. But he could not teach the other men in Plantation how to build a trap from loose ends. Not through the wall, certainly, and probably not even if he had been able to talk to them face to face. This was the kind of skill that Hall had acquired over a lifetime.

But he was able to tell the men in the other cells how to improvise plaster out of brick dust and water and use that to seal some of the holes that the rats used as passageways between cells. The other POWs went to work plastering the rat holes, and for a while, this worked as well as all of Hall's ideas.

But the rats were not pushovers. They began to gnaw their way through the weak plaster barricades, and soon it was a struggle to replaster the holes faster than the rats could gnaw them open again. Once more, Hall came through.

The Vietnamese grew a kind of bell-shaped pepper, which they ate with their rations. The pepper was fiercely hot, hotter than any jalapeño that any American had ever eaten. It was possible for the POWs to sneak one or two of these peppers from the mess hall when they were on food detail, but most of them didn't bother. The peppers were too hot for them to eat and certainly not worth the risk of punishment.

Through the wall, Hall advised the other prisoners to try sticking these peppers into the rat holes to plug them. A day or two later the men noticed that the rats had tried gnawing through the new plugs but had given up before they broke through. The peppers were too hot even for them.

The rats remained a problem — there were no complete, unequivocal victories for the POWs — but Tom Hall had made it into a fight, and the POWs got their innings.

Housekeeping was humdrum stuff for men accustomed to flying supersonic fighters and turning their dirty uniforms over to a laundry run by enlisted men. But it became critical in Plantation and the other camps. The camp was dirty, and sanitation was nonexistent. Spiders, cockroaches, and flies were everywhere. One man tapped out a message designating the housefly the national bird of North Vietnam. Keeping clean was important for its own sake, and because it represented a challenge, however small. It wasn't the stuff of a fighter pilot's dreams, like shooting down a MIG, but under the circumstances it was vital.

Other men, too, had useful ideas, especially about health and hygiene. In their weakened condition, the men in Plantation were easy victims of all sorts of infections and parasites. They worked hard at keeping their cells, their clothes, and themselves clean. Each man was issued a small bar of lye soap every week — it seemed to be almost as abundant as pumpkins — and they washed their uniforms vigorously when they were taken out to bathe.

But they still got sick. Medical lore was dredged up from memory and passed through the wall. When you had diarrhea, you should drink only the broth from your soup and leave any greens or meat it might contain. If you were constipated, you should eat whatever solids were in the soup and leave the liquid. It was not much, but it was a regimen, and they followed it.

Boils were a constant, painful problem, as were abscessed gums. One man remembered a doctor telling him an old piece of medical shorthand — "Piss and pus must come out" — so he sneaked razor blades from the shower, which he then used to lance the boils and open the abscesses. It was painful and messy, but it seemed to work.

Many of the men in Plantation had been seriously injured when they ejected, and there was a lot of discussion, through the wall, about how to "treat" those injuries. What could you do about a broken bone that had not been set properly and was healing crooked?

Stafford's upper arm seemed to be mending, after a fashion. But he could not raise his arm to the level of his chest or move it laterally beyond the arc of about thirty degrees. He improvised slings or used his good arm for support in an attempt to keep the bad one immobilized. This, however, only seemed to increase the stiffness. He imagined himself returning home — whenever that day came — as a cripple.

Down the line of cells somewhere, another POW learned about Stafford's problem and tapped back that he should begin exercising the arm as much as possible to prevent muscle atrophy and to break up the deposits of calcium that were forming around the break. It was something he'd learned after a football injury.

This led to a debate within Stafford's cell. Should he exercise the arm, specifically, and should prisoners exert themselves in general? Dick Stratton, never a man for fitness regimes even before he was shot down, was against strenuous exercise programs. In the case of Stafford's arm, he thought activity would merely aggravate the injury. In the case of other men, exercise would burn calories, and they could not afford to waste a single BTU. They were on starvation rations; sit-ups and push-ups would only exhaust whatever small reserves they had. But Stratton was careful not to overexert his authority on this matter. He did not order the men *not* to exercise strenuously but merely recommended against it. (Later he began exercising himself.)

At first Stafford tried some simple flexing movements. How much worse, he asked himself, could they make his arm? So he would raise it, tentatively, until he reached the point where pain told him to stop. Then he would raise the arm another inch or two, stopping when he could hear something inside begin to tear. It sounded almost like a piece of paper gently ripping. Tears would fill Stafford's eyes, and he would feel himself growing faint. He would lower his arm until the pain had passed and he had regained his breath. Then he would slowly raise his arm again, until he reached the same point, and then he would bite down on his back teeth and go another inch, and one more . . .

After a couple of weeks he noticed that the arc of mobility had grown by a couple of degrees. So he massaged the arm and kept on. He set goals. Get the arm loose enough so that he could use it to drink a cup of water. Then enough so that he could touch the top of his head. Every day he would work the arm until he could hear that sound of tearing paper and he was on the edge of passing out.

The other men in the cell would look away while he was

exercising. Now and then one would say, "How's the arm, Al?"

"Better. Lots better. I can touch my nose."

"That's great, man. Really great. Hang in there."

Other prisoners who did not agree with Dick Stratton's notions about exercise and were desperate for some kind of physical activity began doing calisthenics. This was tricky, since the sound of a man running in place or counting off push-ups would alert the guards. They would open the little judas window to the cell, wave a finger at the man, and tell him to stop. If he were caught repeatedly, he might be taken up to the Big House for interrogation and punishment. Prisoners were expected to sit quietly in their cells, eat their two bowls of soup a day, come out for a bath and a shave once a week, and otherwise do nothing.

So prisoners who wanted to perform calisthenics had to depend on the clearing system and do their exercises when the guards were not close by. When a heavy thud sounded along the wall, they would scramble up from the floor to sit on their bunks, with their hands folded in their laps, like subdued children waiting silently in church for services to begin. Between the warning thuds they knocked out their push-ups and their sit-ups and kept meticulous records of their repetitions. Scores were tapped through the wall, and competitions inevitably followed.

The sit-up count reached into the thousands. A man would fold his blanket into the shape of an exercise mat and get down on the floor, on his back, and begin knocking them out, with the easy rhythm of a metronome, up and back, up and back, up and back. Breathe in, breathe out. Breathe in, breathe out. Soon the steady, repetitious flexing of his own body would shut out everything else, and he would be alert to nothing except movement and the possible thump from a man in another cell, clearing. Up and down . . . six hundred, six hundred one . . . two. Time seemed to slide by when a man was doing his sit-ups. And when he finished, or had to quit, he would feel a kind of overall exhaustion that seemed so much better than the angry tension that grew tighter and tighter inside, like a rope being slowly twisted, when he simply sat on his bunk, hands folded in his lap, waiting for time to pass, feeling his life go by, leaving behind it a trail of . . . nothing.

For some men merely doing calisthenics was insufficient. After thousands of push-ups, tens of thousands of sit-ups, miles of running in place, they wanted something more challenging. For some reason it seemed essential to start lifting weights.

There were, of course, no weights available in Plantation — nothing in the cells that came close. The sawhorses and the pallets that the prisoners used for sleeping were no good — too big and cumbersome. Aside from that, the only thing in the cell was the buckets.

So the physical fitness fanatics in Plantation began curling buckets full of human waste to develop their arms. Some days the buckets were heavy and some days they were light. They always stank, but that seemed less and less important to men who had learned to share space with rats and sit on those buckets with absolutely no privacy. They did their curls, concentrating to make the lifting movement smooth and fluid so the contents of the buckets would not slop around too much inside or spill over the edges.

Years later, when he was home, one of the men went to a movie about weightlifting and body building called *Pumping Iron*. It occurred to him that hour after hour, day after day, for almost six years of his life, what he had been doing was pumping shit. It seemed the perfect description.

It was not enough to work on housekeeping, health, and fitness. Even after you had done all you could to keep the cell, and yourself, clean, exercised until you were exhausted, and taken your turn tapping or clearing, there were still long, empty stretches of time, a void that had to be filled somehow. Somehow you had to keep your mind occupied. Otherwise you would dwell on your situation and sink into a swamp of self-pity. The POWs found they had more resources than they could have imagined for keeping themselves diverted. It came down to discovering what they already knew.

Stafford was on the wall one day when someone from the next cell tapped out a riddle. You are on a path, the message read, and you come to a place where the path goes off in two directions. There is a guard at the head of each new path. If you take one path, you will meet certain death. If you take the other path, you will live. One guard always lies, and the other always tells the truth. You do not know which is which, and you may ask only one question of one of them in order to learn the path to safety. What is the question that will allow you to proceed safely?

It took a long time for the man in the next cell to tap out that message. Much longer for Stafford, who had never been good at math and logic and the other empirical disciplines, to figure out the answer. Months, in fact. But this was the point. When one of his roommates who knew the answer tried to coach him, Stafford said, "No, goddammit. Don't *ruin* it. I'll get it."

Like virtually all of the prisoners, Stafford finally gave up and asked someone to tell him the answer, which was simplicity itself. You ask either guard, "If I ask the other guard which is the road to safety, what will he tell me?" And then you take the opposite path. This was the best of many brain teasers that went through the wall. There were dozens of others.

Killing time was not an altogether new experience for these

aviators. There had always been time to fill while they were waiting to fly, especially in the days before the war. One way of killing that time had been with card games that could be put down before takeoff and then resumed after the mission had been flown and the planes were back down. Ready room and alert room bridge games could last for weeks.

It took some resourcefulness to get a rubber going in prison, when all four players were in different, and not always adjacent, cells. But the players had time to come up with the necessary solutions.

First, you needed cards. The Vietnamese were not handing any out. (They were included in Red Cross and other packages sent to the POWs but were not distributed until very late in the war.) So the POWs had to make them.

Toilet paper was available. A quill could be made from broom straw, ink from ashes and water. The cards were made small so they could be easily concealed.

Next came the fundamental problem of how to play the game. The men who decided to make up a bridge foursome would arrange their cards in the same order. Then the instructions for shuffling would be tapped through each wall. Sometimes these instructions would be relayed by a man who did not play bridge but was willing to help keep the game going and do a little tapping to pass the time.

> CUT DECK TEN CARDS DEEP.
> CUT LARGE PILE FIFTEEN CARDS DEEP.
> PLACE THIRD ON FIRST PILE.

And so on until the deck was shuffled. Then every man would deal four hands, pick up the one that was his, and begin the bidding. Once the bidding was complete, the dummy hand would be turned over. The other hands would remain face down, and as a card was played, the man making the play would tap the card and its place in the original pile so that the other players could find it without looking at the other cards in the hand. It would have been easy to cheat without being caught but also, under the circumstances, utterly pointless. A hand of bridge that might take ten minutes to play under normal conditions could last for two or three weeks when every play had to be tapped through several walls.

Now and then a new man would decline an invitation to play cards, saying that it couldn't be done. Tapping all the bidding and the rounds and the score keeping through several walls would just take too much time. The other men had an answer, which went back to a time when Dick Stratton had been thrown into a totally darkened cell for punishment.

Stratton had been kept in that cell for nearly six weeks. Light deprivation is known to cause severe disorientation and, eventually, a total loss of control — insanity. Stratton's only lifeline was the wall and the man on the other side, Jack Van Loan. At first, simply to give Stratton some kind of reference point, Van Loan would estimate the passage of time and give Stratton a hack every fifteen minutes. It was something.

Then, as time went on, Van Loan began asking Stratton to explain things to him. Books that Stratton had read, courses that he had taken in college, anything that he could remember and describe in detail. Eventually they came to the subject of philosophy, and Stratton was trying to tell Van Loan, through the wall, about a course that he had taken in existentialism. That word, alone, was tough, and Van Loan missed it several times. Each time Stratton would patiently tap it out again. Then, when they had finally gotten that single word straight, Stratton began tapping out the name Kierkegaard. It seemed to take hours.

At one point Stratton tapped out an apology:

SORRY THIS IS TACING SO LONG.

Van Loan tapped back:

DONT WORRY ABT IT. I THINC TIME IS ON OUR SIDE.
CEEP TALCING.

So from then on, whenever a man would protest that a
bridge game would take too long to tap through several walls
of the warehouse, the man on the other side would tap back:

THATS OCAY. TIME IS ON OUR SIDE.

Card games and chess were good for filling time, but they
were not enough to engage fully the minds of college-edu-
cated men who were accustomed to learning as a routine
discipline. So they began memorizing lines from poems or
plays that a man might have been taught to recite as a child
and never forgotten, even if he did not realize that until
now and had to work hard at the job of recall. When he had
the lines, a man in one cell would tap out "Danny Deever"
or "Invictus" to a man in the next cell, who recited them
over and over until he had memorized them himself. The
music of the lines, the hard cadences — especially of Kip-
ling — provided a kind of solace.

> For it's Tommy this and Tommy that
> And Tommy how's your soul?
> But it's thin red line of heroes
> When the drums begin to roll.

Men who had never cared much for poetry began to crave
the verses as they came through the wall. The POWs in one
cell had been learning "The Highwayman," line by pain-
staking line, when they were ordered to move. The order
came just as they were reaching the climax of the poem and
Bess was prepared to "shatter her breast in the moonlight"
to warn the Highwayman. It was like losing a mystery novel
when you are three or four chapters from the end. From
their new cell, which had no common wall and could not

receive messages by tap code, the men smuggled a message asking what had happened.

A message was smuggled back to them — at some risk. It read:

HIGHWAYMAN AND BESS — KIA.

As in some old, preliterate society, storytelling became an important art. The stories and myths of their generation were often films, so after the evening meal and the order to put up the nets and lie down on the hard wooden pallets, it would be time for movies. A man who could remember a film would lie on his bunk and begin patiently narrating the action, scene by scene, going into character for dialogue and adding as much detail to the physical descriptions as he could remember or invent. Many of the POWs had favorite movies they had seen more than once, so they were able to relate a passable summary. Some had a real talent for the work and, with the help of other men who had seen the movie, could assemble a fairly complete account. Certain movies became favorites. *Dr. Zhivago* was easily the best-loved movie in Plantation.

Still, there were long stretches of dead, empty time when nothing happened and a man was reduced to simple mute awareness of his situation. He was hungry. In the summer he was hot and eaten up with skin infections, cold and shivering in the winter. He was desperately uncertain about the future. He did not know if he would be hauled out for a quiz in ten minutes or still be a captive in ten years.

So almost all of the POWs learned to fantasize.

There was a distinction, however, between idle daydreaming and disciplined fantasizing. No one needed to be told that simply crawling under a blanket and dreaming childhood dreams of mother and dog and painless innocence was unhealthy. That kind of random, formless escape would lead a man further and further into passivity, self-pity, and isolation.

So when you fantasized, you tried to create real situations and solve real problems. Properly done, a good session of fantasizing would make you tired and leave you with a sense of having accomplished something.

Al Stafford had always loved to sail, so he would sit up straight with his eyes closed and imagine himself out on the Chesapeake somewhere. He would decide on the season and then try to remember just what the prevailing weather would be. In the summer, when the cell was stifling and full of bugs, he would picture himself out on the bay in winter, when the water was the color of lead, the wind blowing whitecaps off the tops of the swells. He would be wearing oilskins, and except for a lone freighter moving up the ship channel, he would have the bay to himself. In the winter, while he huddled under his blanket, he would imagine himself stripped down to a bathing suit. Crab boats and pleasure sailors would be scattered across the mild green expanse of the bay.

Then he would decide where the wind was coming from and how strong it should be. He would visualize the boat he was sailing. How was it rigged? What sort of sail did it carry? How responsive was it? How much water did it draw?

All right, then. If a strong east wind was blowing at twelve to twenty knots and he was alone in a sloop, on a broad reach, and he had to change tacks, should he take the short way and jibe or the safer solution and come all the way about?

When he set up these problems, Stafford would force himself to be honest and recognize when he made a mistake. It was important to be strict in these matters, to be precise in all the details, and to follow the consequences of each decision ruthlessly so that he learned from his mistakes. Every day he changed the weather and tried to put up just the right amount of sail and pick exactly the right tack. He was never perfect, could always do a little better.

He designed boats for every body of water he had ever sailed, for cruising and for racing. He experimented single-handing big boats and decided that it was too much work. Tried smaller and smaller boats for cruising until he had established the optimum size for a two-week cruise by himself or with someone along to help. As the months passed, he learned the personality of his boat and just what he could expect from it under different conditions. He knew how quickly it would respond and how much sail it could carry in a storm. He learned to sail by the sound of the wind in the rigging and the feel of the rudder in his hand. When everything was just right, his boat felt the way a plane did when it was perfectly trimmed and would fly straight and level if you took your hand off the stick and your feet off the pedals. Of course, when the wind changed, you had to retrim, and if it changed enough, you had to adjust sail. But you learned not to overcorrect.

At the end of an hour or two of sailing, Stafford could taste the salt on his lips and feel the sun on his skin. He sailed for hours and hours. He used real checkpoints and kept a real logbook. "Five knots equals a mile every twelve minutes . . . I'll be at the Oxford lighthouse at 1610 . . ."

In a cell farther down the warehouse another man played golf. He would spend two hours a day playing a course he remembered hole by hole. He would concentrate so hard on his shots that he would feel the tick of the ball when he made contact with the sweet spot. When his mind wandered a little, he would feel the ugly, metallic sensation all the way up his arms and into his shoulders. A goddamned duck hook, he would tell himself, and trudge off into the rough, hoping that he could find his ball and learn not to use too much right hand.

During his golf game his cellmates would leave him alone. It was easy to know that he was playing because he would be sitting on his sleeping pallet, in something like the lotus position, with his eyes closed and his lips moving, just slightly, as he talked himself through the round. Then, after a couple of hours, he would open his eyes and begin to stretch, as if to relieve the tension.

One of the other men in the room would say, "How'd you hit 'em today, Jerry?"

"Not bad. I was two under when I made the turn, but I pushed my drive on fifteen, a long par five. Had to play safe out of the rough and double-bogied the hole. Then I three-putted seventeen from twelve feet out. Really blew it. So I was one over for the round."

"That's not bad."

"No, it was a good round. Great weather, too."

"So what about the handicap?"

"I'm still sitting on a two."

"Little more time on the driving range and you'll be a scratch golfer."

"Putting green is more like it. That one three-putt killed me."

There was only one limit to this kind of fantasizing: you had to know enough about the situation or the task to make it realistic. You could not simply decide you were going to be a professional golfer and imagine yourself in a playoff against Jack Nicklaus if you had never played a round in your life. But if you put yourself into a world that you did know and understand, and you took your time and forced your mind to follow the consequences of every single choice all the way out, then you could create a world of almost tangible reality.

It was escape of a kind. But it was also a discipline. If you were a golfer and you "played" every day, you might feel yourself actually getting better. Although he had not seen blue water for two years, since the morning he last crossed the coast of Vietnam at twenty thousand feet, Al Stafford felt sure that he was a better sailor than he had been when he was shot down. He knew so much more now. He had been through certain situations so many times, in his mind, that he now did the right thing automatically. It was like the time you spent in a flight simulator, on the ground, which prepared you for the situations you later encountered in the air.

But even if it was a means of escape as well as a way to make some productive use of long, empty stretches of time, fantasy was still no substitute for the real thing. When it was too hot and he was too dispirited even to fantasize successfully, Stafford wondered when he would see blue water and feel the wind again. Or, in his worst moments, if he ever would.

Along the row of rooms in the warehouse, men strained to keep busy, finding the solution in everything from a serious form of make-believe to the most elaborate improvisation. A man named Charles Plumb "played" music on the keyboard of a piano diagramed in brick dust on the floor. He would patiently play the pieces he could remember, practicing over and over until he could get them right. Like Tom Hall, Plumb was an innovator. He had grown up in rural Kansas, where he had been an active Boy Scout and 4-H member. Like many boys his age, he had also fooled around with ham radios and had once sent away for a kit to build his own receiver. He remembered enough about the components and the theory that he decided to attempt building a radio in Plantation so that he could listen to news from some source other than Radio Hanoi.

The yard at Plantation was littered with scrap and debris.

On his way to the kitchen to make coal balls or pick up the soup for distribution, Plumb would walk in the typical prisoner fashion, shuffling his feet with his head lowered as if in permanent dejection. Actually, he was looking for wire. He easily found enough for an aerial and a ground.

During interrogations, prisoners used pencils to write out confessions or letters of apology to the camp commander. They routinely pressed too hard and broke the lead. While the guard was sharpening the pencil, they would sneak the small piece of broken lead into their clothing and smuggle it back into their cell. An eighth of an inch of pencil lead set into a sliver of bamboo made a wonderful, highly prized writing instrument. The POWs would carefully hide their pencils against the possibility of a search. Being caught with a pencil was to risk punishment for breaking the camp rule against contraband. Worse, the pencil would be confiscated.

For his radio, Plumb used one of these small pencil points as a detector, balancing it on the edges of two razor blades. For the antenna coil, he wrapped wire around a spool that he made from scrap wood, which he "turned" to shape by rubbing it against the rough wall of the cell. He built a capacitor from alternating sheets of wax paper and aluminum foil smuggled from the kitchen or saved from cigarette packages.

This left the earpiece, which required an electromagnet, diaphragm, and housing. A nail served for the electromagnet. The housing was an unused insulator, stuck in the wall and probably dating back to the time when the French built the camp. He had worked the insulator loose from the wall and was preparing to wrap the nail with fine wire when the guards conducted a search and confiscated all the parts to his radio. He was taken to the Big House, put in the ropes, and forced to write a letter of apology to the camp commander. He never heard the Voice of America on his little radio.

While Plumb was busy with one of his projects, his roommate, Danny Glenn, concentrated on designing and building his dream house. Glenn had studied architecture at Oklahoma State before he went into the navy and was shot down four days before Christmas 1966. In Plantation he filled the hours working on the plans and blueprints for the house he promised himself he would build — exactly to his specifications, with exactly the materials he wanted — when he finally got out of North Vietnam and went home. He would rough out the plans on the floor, carefully working out the dimensions and noting the placement of headers, joists, and studs. Then he would draw up his materials list room by room. His lists were exhaustive and specific, down to the precise gauge of the electric wire. The blueprint of a room would stay on the floor for days, then weeks, while he made his corrections and pondered his decisions.

Lying under his mosquito net at night, Plumb would frequently be awakened by the sound of his cellmate's voice.

"Hey, Charlie?"

"Yeah."

"You asleep?"

"No."

"Listen, if I'm bothering you . . ."

"That's okay. What is it?"

"Well, you know that upstairs bathroom, the little one at the head of the stairs?"

"Uh huh."

"Well, I've been thinking about it and I've decided to go with Mexican tile. What do you think?"

"I think it would look real good."

"You sure?"

"Absolutely."

"It's not too fancy?"

"No. I'd say Mexican tile would be just right."

"Well, what about the color?"

"Hell, I don't know."

"I was thinking green. That dark green like you see on sports cars. British racing green they call it."

"I think that would look real good."

"Okay, Charlie. Thanks a lot."

"Sure."

"Good night."

In the morning Glenn would go to his blueprints and materials list and write in green Mexican tile for the upstairs bathroom. Then he would check the dimensions and do the arithmetic to calculate just how many three-inch squares he would need and where he would have to cut to fit. He would memorize as much as he could and make notes in tiny script on a piece of paper from a cigarette package, using one of the contraband pencil leads or an improvised pen. Then he would fold the sheet into the smallest possible square and hide it in a crack in the wall, erase the schematic of the room he'd been working on, and start another.

That night, after the mosquito nets were down, he would say softly, "Charlie, I'm thinking about paneling that family room downstairs. What do you think . . . ?"

Nine

ONE MORNING, late in the summer of 1968, the guards came to Warehouse One and motioned for Bob Sawhill and Arv Chauncey to "roll it up." This signal, which they made by spinning their hands, meant that the men were to put everything they owned into their sleeping mats, which they then rolled up and tucked under their arms for the move to a new cell, or even a new camp. The POWs didn't have much — blanket, towel, toothbrush, soap, clay water pot, and a tin drinking cup — so it took only a minute or two to roll it up. And the guards were in a hurry. They did not allow the men to speak to one another. No good-bye handshakes, no "See you later, babe." The men who were leaving managed a slight nod. Stratton and Stafford nodded back. And then the door closed and they were alone.

"Looks like just you and me for a while," Stafford said.

"Looks like."

They would remain alone there for almost a year.

Their immediate response to this new situation was to get on the wall and try to find out as much as they could about what was going on. *What is the significance of . . . ?*

The Vietnamese did not follow any pattern or logic in these things. Men were moved without cause, and more often than not, the moves changed nothing of importance. Some men were glad to have new cellmates or to leave one camp for another. Almost any change in the oppressive routine, the essential *sameness* of things, was welcomed. But, even in change, things remained the same. Numbingly so.

This had been part of a major shakeup. Chauncey and Sawhill — along with several others, including Charlie Plumb — had been taken out of Plantation and moved to another camp called the Zoo. Several men who had been at the Zoo were now brought into Plantation. Every new man had to be identified and debriefed for names. Who are you? Where have you been? What are the names of other Americans you have actually seen and touched? What are the names of Americans you have heard about?

Gathering all this information took time, a month or more, so Stafford and Stratton had this to keep them busy. Stratton was still senior, and Stafford served as his deputy. Together they purged and updated their list of names, got the orders about Bouncing Back to the new men, and learned what they could about other camps, recent war news, and any other information that might be useful or merely interesting. Gradually the dust from the big shakeup settled, and Stafford and Stratton fell back into the grind of resisting both the North Vietnamese and the more subtle tortures of monotony, uncertainty, and despair.

There was marginally more for each man to do now that they were just two. If one man was tapping, then the other had to clear. That job could not be spread around. Nor could the small housekeeping chores; but this was almost a gift. Any job was a release of sorts. Such camp chores as there were — making coal balls, emptying buckets, picking up the soup — were considered prizes, and when the men in one cell were repeatedly given these jobs, the other POWs got on the wall and asked Stratton to protest to the camp commander, which he did. (While the POWs had tried to keep the identity of the senior man secret for a while, this proved impossible.) If given the opportunity, most POWs would eagerly have done hard manual labor — breaking rocks, planting rice, pulling weeds — anything to leave those cells and get out from under the crushing weight of empty time.

So while they were a little busier, Stratton and Stafford now had less to divert them. Chauncey had told long, rambling stories about fishing trips in the Cascade Mountains with his two young sons. Bob Sawhill, the gentleman fighter pilot who could remember and describe planes he had flown, meals he had eaten, and women he had dated all over the world, was also gone. This left a vacuum in the room, the sort that one feels in a family when a child leaves home for the first time.

It would be difficult for Stratton and Stafford to fill that vacuum. Better, in a way, if they had both been moved and had new cellmates. They had heard each other's stories for months now, and there was not much left in reserve. In some way they had used each other up.

Also, Stratton and Stafford were temperamentally very different men. If they had been in the same squadron, they probably would have been cordial but not friendly.

Al Stafford was a voluble man, a talker and an extrovert, squadron spark plug and cheerleader. If some of the boys were going out to the O-Club for a few drinks, he would be there, lifting stingers and telling stories until the bar closed. He was emotional, almost high-strung. When things went bad, he got down. When things went right, he was sky high.

Richard Stratton was the opposite. A devout Roman Catholic from a working-class family in Quincy, Massachusetts, he was something of a loner and a grind as fighter pilots go. The ordeal that culminated in the famous bowing episode had only deepened his reserve. He tried not to get too high nor sink too low. His role as SRO in Plantation, the responsibility for coordinating resistance at a camp where cooperation was rewarded with early release, made him even more grave and serious. He was a deeply sober and religious man.

While they might have gone their own ways in the fleet, in Plantation Stratton and Stafford had no choice. Stafford was still recovering from his wounds; Stratton was sick with amoebic dysentery. Neither man was in shape for emotional combat or even petty skirmishing. They went out of their way to respect each other's moods, silences, and habits. Getting along was another piece of the survival strategy, and they both worked on it. Stratton was a brooder and could sit for hours on his bunk, utterly silent and motionless, thinking about things he simply did not feel like sharing. Stafford had to respect that, just as Stratton respected and tolerated Stafford's pacing and his nervous talk.

Without realizing it, each man began to match his strengths to the other's needs; they became an emotional team of sorts, the same way they teamed up to remember names and to clear while one man tapped or to take an extra turn emptying buckets or sweeping the room when the other had been up to the Big House and come back exhausted and in pain.

Al Stafford had never been much for books. He was acutely aware of this and considered it a deficiency. He had left St. John's before he earned his degree, and the lack of a degree bothered him. It was a gap that he intended to fill someday, but he couldn't do much about it in Hanoi.

He felt this lack even more keenly rooming with Stratton, who had left Quincy for Washington, D.C., and Georgetown University with only enough money to enroll for one semester — money that he had saved himself, not his parents' money. Stratton spent six years working his way through Georgetown. He would leave for a semester to work as a page on Capitol Hill. For half a year he lived on peanut butter. But he had finally graduated with a degree in political science, and that degree was important to him. He was a man who read books and took ideas seriously. He had taken the Jesuit example to heart and was quick and formidable in argument. In the ready room Stafford might have found this intimidating — or boring — and stayed away. But in Plantation there was no shame and no covering your deficiencies. Vanity was a luxury. Stafford decided to learn what he could from Stratton. There was no alternative, and besides, it gave Stratton pleasure to talk about what he knew.

One morning, after the soup, when the wall was quiet and there was no activity in the yard and they were simply sitting on their pallets silently waiting out the time, Stafford said, "Dick, you are obviously a religious man. I see you praying and I've heard you talk about God and faith and the rest of it."

"Yeah."

"Well, let me ask you something, if you don't mind."

"What?"

"Well, I don't mean to be smart ass or anything . . . I honestly want to know, okay?"

"All right. But what is it?"

"Well, I mean, *how* do you know there is a God?"

Stratton straightened up on his pallet. "In the first place, there is nothing wrong with the question, obviously. It's the first question. Everything else follows."

And with that, Stratton went on to explain Aquinas' five proofs for the existence of God. Stafford remembered hearing them before, in an introductory philosophy class when his mind was miles away and he felt like some kind of prisoner. Now that he really was a prisoner, he found it remarkably easy to pay attention. Stratton went on for two or three hours, explaining the order of efficient causes, eternity, infinite perfection — everything he could remember from the *Summa Theologica*.

For the next few weeks Stafford asked questions and Stratton answered them. The two men discussed theology with the kind of detachment and rationality that would have pleased a Jesuit. They were not trying to convert each other or destroy each other's convictions so much as trying to learn and to maintain their mental agility.

Stafford could not play William of Occam or Voltaire in these discussions; had no real desire to. For him the point was education, and while he was not argued out of his skepticism, he felt that he was learning something he needed to learn, that he was filling the gap in his education. He did not feel defensive or resentful. In fact, he felt a kind of gratitude, and with it the desire to repay Stratton in kind.

He did not have any theology to give in return, but he wasn't entirely without resources. He began to dig into his memory, using his increased powers of recall. He had spent hundreds of hours sitting alone and thinking, trying to remember the events of his life: books he had read, dialogue from the plays that he had seen, the names of all his teachers, his classmates, the women he had dated. He discovered that if he concentrated, really *worked* at it, pushed himself past the point where recall was fun or amusing and made it into a challenge, then he could remember things that he had no idea he even knew. Recall, he discovered, was like a muscle, and the more he worked it and exercised it, the stronger it got. When he wanted to remember something and couldn't, he told himself to bear down, goddammit, and work harder. It was there; he just needed to dig for it.

Like everyone at St. John's, he had taken courses in Latin and Greek. He had treated those courses like all the others, learning just enough, cramming for tests and then forgetting until it came time for the next exam. If there was anything in this world that he would not need to know, he believed, it was some dead language.

Now, in Warehouse One, he worked to recall some of those ancient words in order to teach them to Stratton. He worked at it, going deeper and deeper until the process was almost physically painful and his head would ache with the strain. Finally, after weeks of effort, he had remembered enough to be able to teach Stratton the opening verse of the Book of John in Greek.

Stories about his life came more easily to Stafford, and if he was curious about the things Stratton had learned, then Stratton was eager to know about the things Stafford had done. If Stratton was the professor in their cell, then Stafford was the raconteur. Stafford was surprised to learn that he'd lived a colorful life.

"Dick, did I ever tell you about how I played in the minstrel show?"

"The *what?*"

"Minstrel show."

"Never heard of it."

"You *never* heard of a minstrel show?"

"Nope. What is it?"

"Well . . . ," and for the next several days Stafford would explain about Shufflefoot and Mr. Bones and the role of the interlocutor and describe how he played clarinet and saxophone as a teenager.

He told Stratton about duck hunting on the Eastern Shore of Maryland and described the proper method of building a brush blind and laying out a set of decoys. Told him how, during the season, the boys in his high school would get up before dawn to go hunting and would come to school still wearing their hunting clothes and carrying their shotguns.

"What the hell would you do with a shotgun in school?"

"Put it in your locker and leave it there until school was over. Then take it home and clean it."

"You're kidding."

"No."

"Amazing. What if you killed some ducks? What would you do with *them?*"

"Put them in your locker with your shotgun. After school you'd take them home and clean them, too. Do you know the best way to get the pinfeathers out of a duck? Well, . . ."

Stafford would tell these stories hour after hour, searching for the compelling detail or the single item of expertise that would establish his credibility: the best way to anchor a brush blind, caulk a skiff, protect a shotgun against rust.

Stratton listened when Stafford told stories. Stafford listened when Stratton talked about the nature of faith. When one tired of listening, the other stopped talking. They respected silences as much as they respected words, treating each other with a kind of deference that sometimes reminded Stafford of couples who have been married for years and know how to anticipate each other's moods. It was the strangest goddamned thing. He could not remember spending even a small fraction of the time he had spent with Stratton in the close company of another human being. He had never been anything like this familiar, even *intimate,* with anyone else. And the strangest thing was, there was never any trouble. No arguments, no sulks, no little ego clashes or pissing contests. If the war did go on for another five years or even — hard to think it — ten, fifteen, *twenty* . . . well, if that was what happened, there was nothing that he could do about it. But if it had to be, then he couldn't ask for a better cellmate than Dick Stratton.

But Stratton often ran out of things to say, or the desire to say them. And while the business of running the camp —

passing messages, updating the list of names, circulating the news — ate up hundreds of hours, there were times when everything that could be done had been done and there was an empty silence in Warehouse One.

Stratton had an uncommon ability to sit out these long, vacant stretches, lost in his thoughts while he waited for the next event or the next piece of camp business that required his attention. Stafford lacked this gift. But he discovered a lifeline in the form of a half-inch hole in the wall between his cell and the next in line.

The hole had been drilled for a pipe that either had never been installed or had been removed for other uses by the Vietnamese and had never been plastered over, perhaps because it was so small that it was impossible to imagine any use to which POWs could put it. Or maybe it was simply an oversight. Whatever the reason, the hole was cut through the wall at the height of Stafford's chin, making it perfect for looking into the next cell and, better, talking to someone on the other side.

The someone was Ben Ringsdorf, an air force captain from Elba, Alabama, a tiny town in the southeastern portion of the state known as the Wiregrass. Elba was the home of the Dorsey Company, maker of truck trailers; otherwise it was merely an anonymous town supported by agriculture and timber, the sort of place where young men grow up dreaming of the day when they will leave and go on to lives of adventure and glory.

Stafford and Ringsdorf began using the small hole in the wall to pass spare cigarettes back and forth. The prisoners were given a few harsh Vietnamese cigarettes every day, and lighting up became an event. Stafford and Ringsdorf eventually began standing at the hole while they smoked, talking to each other in the usual way, beginning with shootdown stories and then falling into detailed biography. They talked for a few minutes at first. Within weeks they were at the wall for hours at a time, alternately talking and listening. For some reason they never seemed to run out of things to talk about. They spent hours talking about the most commonplace topics — the way the town of Elba was laid out and how the roads led out of town, one of them to a bridge that crossed the river, and the way the bridge sounded when you drove across it and it groaned under the weight of your car — but the aimlessness of the conversation did not bother either man. They were merely hanging out together and bullshitting to pass the time, although neither man knew what the other looked like. Ringsdorf called it "chunking trash," and Stafford understood the southern idiom perfectly.

Ringsdorf and Stafford had similar sensibilities; if they had been in a squadron together, they would have been friends. Neither was as serious or grave as Dick Stratton. They liked jokes, any kind of jokes, and they told each other every joke they had ever heard and could remember.

In a week or two they had exhausted their store of jokes, so they began telling jokes disguised as stories. Ideally, the man listening would not know that he was hearing a joke until the punch line was sprung on him. This lasted another few days. There was a finite supply of jokes, and it was exceedingly difficult to make up a good one. They tried and learned that neither of them had the gift.

"I guess that's why we're here," Stafford said, "and not in Hollywood, writing for Bob Hope."

"You like Bob Hope?"

"Sure. I wish I could remember just half of his Bing Crosby jokes."

"Even ten percent."

"Wonder if old Bob will be bringing his show to Hanoi?"

"That might be the only way we'll ever hear some new jokes."

But if jokes were difficult to make up, puns were relatively easy, because it did not matter how bad a pun was. The worse the better, in fact. The more strained and tortured and involved the pun, the more the listener groaned, which was a show of appreciation.

So Stafford and Ringsdorf began to work up elaborate puns to tell each other through the small hole in their common wall. The best way was to begin with some proverb or figure of speech and then work backward, first changing the words of the original aphorism and then inventing some involved story for which the new proverb would serve as the moral. An ill wind blows no good . . . A stitch in time saves nine . . . Early to bed and early to rise. Any figure of speech that could be twisted would work. Stafford and Ringsdorf would spend hours, or days, inventing long, preposterous stories leading up to a moral that would be a reworked proverb. They called these stories Aesop's feebles.

There was no such thing as a bad feeble, unless it was short and obvious, and even then it was appreciated by the other man. Anything to relieve the monotony.

Stafford reworked the aphorism "A penny saved is a penny earned" from *Poor Richard's Almanac.* He invented a character named Benny for his story — this was especially good, since Benny could be Ben Ringsdorf himself. Then he had Benny shave all the hair on his body. At the conclusion of the story, Benny is struck by lightning and reduced to ashes, which are put in a small jar.

The story took days to tell. Finally, at the end, Stafford asked through the small hole, "And you know what the lesson of that story is?"

Ringsdorf thought a moment, but he was stumped.

"No."

"Well, it just goes to show that a Benny shaved is a Benny urned."

Ringsdorf found this hysterical and collapsed on the floor of his cell laughing. He told the story in turn to a man in the next cell through a similar hole in the wall. The man on the other side was Jim Shively, an F-105 pilot, Air Force Academy graduate from the class of 1964 who had gone on to graduate school in international relations at Georgetown. Shively was one of the bright young stars in the air force, a man whose career had looked limitless until he caught a SAM and lost his hydraulics before he could make it to the Laotian mountains and possible rescue.

Stafford, Ringsdorf, and Shively told their feebles hour upon hour. They became known as the punsters. Other POWs who found the whole exercise excruciatingly unfunny called themselves the antipunsters. Punsters constantly tried to trap antipunsters in a kind of low-level intrigue that lasted as long as the war.

For Stafford, those months in Warehouse One, with Stratton as his roommate and Ben Ringsdorf as his neighbor, were a time when he recovered, Bounced Back, more than he would ever have thought possible in the weeks immediately after he was shot down. He felt a bond with those two men — a bond based on gratitude — unlike any he had ever felt with another human. Stratton, a man he might barely have spoken with or gotten to know if they had been together in a peacetime billet, was a source of strength and learning, an example in the way he did his duty and clung stoically to his own values. Ringsdorf, whose face he had never seen, was a sidekick, a buddy, the kind of man with whom he could talk easily for hours about what he had done with his life up to now and what he would do with the rest of his life once he got home. The support of these two men, freely given, made Stafford believe, more than any of the scraps of news coming in from the outside, that he *would* leave Vietnam someday and go home.

*

A few days before Christmas 1968, Stafford and Stratton were taken from their cell to the Big House, where an interrogator told them they would be filmed decorating a room where a few prisoners would be brought in to open packages from home. The opening of the packages would also be filmed. They tried to talk their way out of it, making up various reasons why they were not suitable subjects. There was the matter of their weight, and Stafford's arm still appeared bent and withered. But the interrogator insisted. Before the impasse reached the head-butting stage, Stratton said, "Okay, Al, let's decorate the room for them."

They were put in a room that had been lighted like a movie set. There was a small tree in the room and some tinsel, which they were told to drape on it. While they did this, a stranger with a movie camera recorded the scene. Then they were told to put posters on the wall. The posters were crudely lettered with messages of Peace on Earth and No More War. Again, Stafford and Stratton refused to cooperate. The cameraman stopped filming, and the interrogator lost patience.

"If you do not put the posters on the wall, you will be severely punished."

"I don't know how," Stratton said lamely.

"It is simple," the interrogator said. "Put the finger in the paste," he pointed to a pot of wet glue, "and put the paste on the wall. Then put the poster on the paste."

Stratton looked at Stafford and shrugged. His dark, craggy face was as close to a smile as Stafford had ever seen it. "All right, Al," Stratton said, "you heard the man. Put 'the finger' in the paste."

"Aye, aye, sir."

So Stafford and Stratton were filmed dutifully using their middle finger to dip paste from the jar and apply it to the posters, which they then plastered to the wall. The interrogator and the cameraman were happy, and so were Stratton and Stafford when they walked back across the courtyard to Warehouse One.

"Merry Christmas," Stratton said, when the door had closed behind them.

"Merry Christmas to you, Dick."

Stratton sat on his bunk trying to imagine Christmas at home with his wife and children. Stafford went to the hole to smoke and tell the story to Ringsdorf, who appreciated it enormously.

The picture of Stratton and Stafford was released by the Vietnamese and appeared in newspapers back in the States, where people saw them putting "the finger" in the paste, and the message came through loud and clear. It was another small, transitory victory.

Ten

LATE IN FEBRUARY 1969 the guards came for Al Stafford and motioned for him to roll it up. He was being moved. He nodded good-bye to Stratton. It was hard leaving, though usually a POW welcomed any change in routine. He thought as he left Warehouse One, with his pitiful goods rolled under his arm, that whatever happened next, he would not ever feel closer to someone he shared space with.

He followed the guard up to the Big House, where an interrogator introduced him to his new roommate, the youngest and, in many ways, the most extraordinary POW in North Vietnam.

Douglas Brent Hegdahl was not an aviator. He was not, for that matter, even an officer. In June 1966, when he was captured, Hegdahl was a twenty-year-old seaman who had been in the navy less than six months, an anonymous enlisted man serving as an ammunition handler on a cruiser in the Gulf of Tonkin. One night Hegdahl had gone up on deck (in violation of orders) to watch the guns fire. He had been stunned by the concussion from a five-incher and fallen overboard. He was not missed until morning, and when the ship reversed course, the lookouts could find no sign of him. The crew was mustered for a memorial service, and the war went on.

Hegdahl had managed to stay afloat all night and was exhausted and close to drowning by dawn, when he was picked up by a Vietnamese fishing junk. The fishermen treated him well, even tried to feed him and make minimal conversation. When they returned to shore, they turned him over to the militia, who put him through the same sort of ordeal they inflicted on pilots who had been shot down. When he refused to provide anything beyond name, rank, service number, and date of birth, he was clubbed senseless with a rifle butt. Eventually he was moved to Hoa Lo, where the interrogators went to work on him.

They plainly — and understandably — did not believe his story, which sounded like something someone, even a spy, might make up or use as a cover. But Hegdahl stuck to it. His interrogators never put him in the ropes, but he was made to stand at attention for hour upon hour, deprived of sleep. Finally, the North Vietnamese seemed to decide that Hegdahl probably was not some kind of plant carrying an escape plan and was instead just what he said he was. He was transferred out of Hoa Lo to the Zoo, where the first American he met was an equally suspicious aviator who thought that Hegdahl might be a Vietnamese plant. Eventually the pilot also decided that Hegdahl's incredible story had to be true.

Hegdahl might have been a mere enlisted man and no great catch for the Vietnamese, but he was no fool. He quickly realized, however, that it was to his advantage to convince his captors that he was exactly that — a helpless, innocent fool, someone they did not have to worry about. When he was asked to write confessions, he agreed, and then asked the Vietnamese how to spell every single word of the statement they wanted him to write. After they had looked up the spelling of more than a dozen words, they gave up and took the pencil and paper away. Hegdahl was treated like a harmless oaf. They gave him the name Tho, which translates as "the innocent one."

In truth he was a resister — one of the best. Better by far than some pilots and professionals who collaborated right up to accepting early release, something that Hegdahl refused.

This occurred in Plantation, where he was sent from the Zoo. On July 11, 1967, Hegdahl met his first roommate at Plantation. This was Dick Stratton, who quickly realized that the young seaman was an asset in his plans and his attempts to organize the camp.

Because the guards did not take him seriously, Hegdahl was able to move around the yard more freely than the other prisoners. When he was on a detail, he could detour off the rigid paths that other prisoners were forced to follow. The Vietnamese indulged him if he took too long in the shower or in the latrine when he was on bucket-dumping detail, or if he wandered aimlessly on his way to the kitchen to make coal balls, or seemed to spend a long time raking or sweeping in the same spot. Hegdahl devised something he called the sweep code, which he used when he was outside an isolated cell with his broom and had a message from Stratton for the prisoners inside. He would sweep in short, rhythmic strokes that spelled out the letters of the message as they appeared in the tap code matrix. Sweep sweep . . . sweep sweep sweep . . . sweep . . . sweep sweep sweep sweep . . .

Hegdahl also used the opportunities his time outside the cell gave him to plant messages from Stratton in various hiding places around the camp. These locations were called mailboxes by the POWs. Mailboxes were as important to the resistance as the tap code, since some cells were isolated and the men in them could not be reached any other way. A loose tile in the latrine might be a good mailbox, for instance. If Hegdahl was dumping buckets and took a little extra time to pry a tile loose and hide a message, the guards would not become suspicious. It was just "Heddle," as they called him, the slow one.

Because he was not watched closely, Hegdahl was also able to scrounge and steal useful items when he was in the kitchen or called up to the Big House for a quiz. He stole cigarettes, paper, pencil points, extra food — anything that might make life a little easier for his fellow prisoners. Sometimes he stole things just for the sake of doing it, because it was a form of resistance. Once he went so far as to pour sand in the gas tank of an interrogator's prized motorcycle that was parked in the yard.

Hegdahl had another skill that was extremely useful to Stratton: a remarkable memory. As the population of Plantation grew, Hegdahl effortlessly added to the list of names he could recall. As new prisoners arrived with reports of other men in other camps, Hegdahl committed the names to his spongelike memory until he could recite more than two hundred and fifty. He was also able to memorize hometowns and the names of wives, where they were available. Stratton quickly realized that the best way to get an authoritative list of names back to the United States was to send Douglas Hegdahl out with a group that the Vietnamese released.

Hegdahl could have gone with the first group. Stratton had realized, during the summer when he and Hegdahl were cellmates, that the Vietnamese were preparing them for release. They were given extra rations and allowed outside for some sun every day, almost as though they were being fattened and tanned in order to make a good impression. It made sense, Stratton decided. Because of the bowing episode, he was an embarrassment to the Vietnamese. Hegdahl was, in his captors' minds, a peasant. Releasing him would be consistent with their theories of class.

Stratton's first impulse had been to frustrate the Vietnamese, so he and Hegdahl began dumping their extra food into their buckets. Pouring a plate of crisp fried potatoes into a bucket of human waste was agony for Hegdahl, who weighed over two hundred pounds when he was captured and had an adolescent fondness for fattening food. But he did it because he was part of the team and those were Stratton's orders.

But Stratton's next orders were even more difficult to obey. He had thought about it and decided that Hegdahl could do more good as an early release than as a resister in the camp.

"Doug," Stratton said, in tones that were even more grave than usual, "if you get the chance, I want you to go home."

"I can't do that," Hegdahl said.

"Yes, you can."

Hegdahl argued that he couldn't fink out on the rest of the prisoners, and, anyway, what about the code?

"I'll take the responsibility," Stratton said.

"I can't do it."

"You can and you will. That's an order. If you have a chance to go home, take it. If it means writing a letter asking for amnesty, then write the letter. You will do a lot more good at home, with the information you have in your head, than you will here."

Hegdahl tried arguing again. Stratton put it in the form of a direct order. "If anyone says anything when you get back, you tell them it was an order from your superior officer. And when I get back, I'll back you up. Now that's all there is to it."

It was not long after that, when Stratton refused to cooperate in the production of some propaganda, that he was taken out of the cell he shared with Hegdahl and put in solitary. His new cell was totally darkened — no light bulb and no windows or gun ports. Stratton could feel the insects and rats that crawled over his body, but he could not see them. He was left in that cell, alone, for nearly six weeks. It was during this ordeal that Stratton received the fifteen-minute time hacks from Jack Van Loan and, in turn, tried to tap what he had learned about existentialism through the wall as a way to hang on to his sanity.

After Stratton was hauled out, Hegdahl spent some time in solitary. He continued to throw away food. Eventually he was moved in with another POW, Air Force Captain Joe Crecca, and persuaded to meet with a delegation that included the antiwar leaders Rennie Davis and Tom Hayden. At one point Hegdahl gave Hayden the finger. Hayden smiled.

This was November 1967. After Hegdahl and Crecca were caught communicating with the men in the next cell, they were separated. Hegdahl was left alone for a few days then moved in with another officer, an Air Force Academy graduate, who was plainly a willing, even eager, candidate for early release. He complained endlessly, so much so that Hegdahl wished he were back in solitary.

In January Hegdahl, his new cellmate, and another badly wounded pilot were taken to the Big House and told that if they wrote to Ho Chi Minh requesting release, they could go home. The pilots wrote their letters. Hegdahl refused. A part of him regretted this impulsive, belligerent decision, not so much because it meant that he would have to stay in Plantation, but because he had violated a direct order and that order had come from Stratton, the man he most respected, next to his father, in the whole world.

In February three POWs, including the one who had refused Stratton's orders in the shower room, left Plantation and Vietnam.

Seaman Hegdahl stayed.

Since then he had continued to play Stepin Fetchit for the

guards and, at the same time, to pass and pick up messages from the mailboxes, scrounge and steal, and memorize names. He was taken out of his cell and driven from Plantation to the coast somewhere and made to act the part of an American being captured at the shore in a propaganda film. He botched the job, take after take, until the cameraman ran out of film. He was driven back to Plantation and thrown in solitary, where he went on a hunger strike. If his picture were ever to show up in a propaganda film, he decided, then he was going to make sure that anyone who studied the film would know exactly what was going on. His weight fell to 120, and when, indeed, his picture did appear in some Japanese film, he looked like a man close to starvation.

Meanwhile, Stratton's order that he accept early release had been countermanded by a new, more senior officer in camp. It now appeared that Hegdahl would be in North Vietnam until the war ended.

Stafford and Hegdahl were given the usual speech by the camp commander — told to obey the rules about communicating with other prisoners, keeping contraband, and so forth — then were led, with their small bundles tucked under their arms, across the courtyard to their new home in a row of cells called the Annex, where they settled in. There was no way to know how long this stretch would be. Weeks, months, perhaps years. The constants in a POW's life were uncertainty, monotony, and fear.

At this stage of the war, spring 1969, the level of fear had dropped almost to manageable proportions. Men were still being hauled up to the Big House for quizzes, and now and then these interrogations turned ugly. But more and more the POWs were learning how to avoid head buttings and the more severe forms of punishment. There had been no bombing around Hanoi for several months now. Negotiations dragged on without progress in Paris. The pall of mutual desperation that once lay over Plantation had been lifted. The POWs and their captors coexisted in sullen harmony. While it was still forbidden to communicate, for instance, the POWs continued to tap and signal and leave messages in their mailboxes. They were careful not to be too blatant, and the guards no longer tried very hard to catch them. Some men in camp were allowed to send out a few letters, and some mail, even a package or two, came in. In this, as in all things, it was impossible to discern a pattern in the way the North Vietnamese did things. Why was one man allowed to write while his cellmate was not? Nobody could say.

If the level of fear had been reduced, then the monotony and uncertainty had risen correspondingly. With no new shootdowns coming in, there was less important information to spread through the communications network, less news coming in from the outside, less reason to believe that the war was nearing a climax.

So Hegdahl and Stafford settled in and began to do the usual things to keep each other diverted. Primarily they told stories, beginning with the inevitable shootdown story.

"Nobody has a shootdown story like mine," Hegdahl told Stafford. "Nobody in Plantation and probably in all of Vietnam. A few months ago we had a high-fast, low-slow contest. You know. Everybody tapped through the wall their altitude and air speed when they were shot down. Some air force guy flying F-104s on MIGCap got hit by a SAM when he was at fifty thousand feet going Mach 1.5 or something. He won the high-fast. I got the low-slow. Fifteen feet of altitude and twenty knots air speed. Nobody else came close."

They talked about the camp and what they had learned

and endured. And they talked about their lives before they became prisoners of this war.

Hegdahl had lived a serene small-town life. His parents owned the hotel in Clark, South Dakota. As he described it, in vivid detail, Stafford could easily picture the weary salesmen who came into Clark, carrying their suitcases full of samples and asking for a room with a bath. Listening to Hegdahl was almost like watching a movie.

"There was an old glass-topped candy counter in the lobby, Al. You know the kind."

Yes, Stafford said, running the movie in his mind. For some reason it seemed to be in black and white.

The wood around the glass was old oak, and the years and years of sunlight had bleached it, Hegdahl said, until it was almost blond. "You know what? We didn't sell much candy, either. There were some Hershey bars that had been in there so long that the sunlight had turned those dark brown wrappers almost white."

There was a crack in the glass, Hegdahl said, and instead of replacing the whole panel, his father had carefully drilled a hole in the glass and then tightened washers down over the hole to keep the crack from widening. The lens of Stafford's eye focused on that lead washer and the cracks that ran like spokes from its center. He could listen to Hegdahl describe that old hotel all day long. And he did, in fact, many days.

Hegdahl also talked about his family. There was something equally simple and blissful about his descriptions of them and the things they did.

"We were always playing jokes, you know, Al. My brother and I especially liked to play jokes on my dad. You know what we did one time?"

"What did you do, Doug?"

"Well, we painted his car."

"Painted it?"

"That's right. Painted that sucker blue."

Stafford, who had not known his father and had been raised by two stern men, couldn't imagine it.

"What did he do?"

"Well, he was pretty surprised. And kind of mad at first. Then we showed him that we'd used water-soluble paint. Washed right off. He thought it was pretty funny then. But we had him going for a while there."

"I can imagine," Stafford said. Though, in truth, he couldn't.

The days passed, and Stafford listened to these stories, and when he grew bored and irritable and began his nervous pacing, Hegdahl would try to think of some new story to tell him. When he couldn't think of a story to tell, he tried to engage Stafford in conversations about what they would do when the war was over and they went home.

One day he broke a long silence by saying, "Al, you know, I think I definitely know what I want to do when I go home to South Dakota."

"What's that, Doug?"

"I'm going to buy some land and farm it."

"Oh yeah?"

"Yeah. Land's pretty cheap around Clark, and I ought to be able to make the payment on what I've saved while I'm in here. I know just the kind of land I want. River bottom, with real rich soil. And you know what I'm going to grow?"

"What?"

"Pumpkins. I'm going to have the finest pumpkin patch in the Dakotas. I'm going to go down to the Ag School and find out what the best hybrid pumpkin seed is and I'm going to buy a few hundred of them. Then I'm going to make my mounds in that rich soil and fertilize it real good with manure and plant those seeds. I'm going to make sure they get plenty of water and I'm going to pinch just enough buds to make sure that the pumpkins I get grow *big*. They'll be the biggest pumpkins around.

"Then I'm going to wait until fall and the first frost, when those pumpkins are ripe and orange. Then you know what I'm going to do?"

"What, Doug?"

"I'm going to go out one night, when the full moon is shining on those pumpkins, and I'm going to have a Louisville Slugger in my hand, and I'm going to beat the living hell out of all those pumpkins."

When he had stopped laughing enough to speak, Stafford said, "Doug, will you call me before you do it? I'll come out and help you. And I'll bring my own bat."

They passed time this way, and the days limped by. Meanwhile, Dick Stratton was trying to persuade the new senior officer who had been transferred into the camp that it was good strategy to get Hegdahl to go with the next group of releases. It was not an easy job, since the new man was in an isolated cell and could be reached only through mailboxes. He was a hard-liner and at first flatly turned Stratton down. "Nobody goes home," he answered in a message left in a mailbox. "Not that kid. Not anybody."

But Stratton was convinced that his plan was sound, and he was a deeply persistent man. He kept sending messages, explaining that Hegdahl had a phenomenal memory. He could effortlessly recite poetry that the POWs had shared. Had learned the Gettysburg Address backwards and forwards. And he had those 260 names down cold. He was the best — and for that matter the only — hope they had for getting those names home.

Eventually Stratton prevailed, and the word was passed through the walls to the cell where Hegdahl and Stafford were struggling against monotony and uncertainty. The new camp SRO officially ordered Hegdahl to accept early release and to go home with those names.

"Al, I can't do that."

"Why not?"

"I can't bug out on the guys." Hegdahl had heard all of the things that were said about the slimies. He had roomed with one man in the first group and could not stand the idea of being like that man, or any of the others who had taken early release. It was insupportable.

Stafford tried to convince him that his leaving was different. Speaking in what he hoped was a fatherly way, he said, "It's not the same with you, Doug. You can understand that."

"I can't go home while the rest of you guys stay here. If one of us goes, then we all go."

"It's an order, Doug."

"I don't care. I'm not going."

So Stafford found himself in the same position that Stratton had been in almost two years earlier.

"All right, Seaman Hegdahl. I am a lieutenant commander and your superior officer . . ."

When Stafford had finished, Hegdahl said, bleakly, "Aye, aye, sir," and that was the end of it. When the next opportunity came, even if he had to write a personal letter to Ho Chi Minh requesting amnesty and apologizing for his crimes against the Vietnamese people and promising never to set foot in the country again (that part would be easy), no matter what it took, Doug Hegdahl was going to do it and take early release and, when he got home, recite his list of names and tell people exactly what was going on.

But before that could happen, the walls caved in.

Eleven

IKE VINES reaching for the light, the men in Plantation —
in fact, all the POWs in Vietnam — took advantage of
any possible opportunity to communicate. Where there
was another prisoner, they tried to find a way to make contact and communicate — *something,* even just a name. Where
they could not say something, write words, or tap out letters
by code, they made a signal. One man whom Stafford later
got to know well had been in Hoa Lo for weeks before he
saw his first American. The other man smiled and gave him
the finger.

"Al," he said to Stafford, "I couldn't believe it. I mean,
here I was, and here is this guy, all bent up from shootdown
wounds. He's carrying a shit bucket with one hand, and with
the other one, he gives me the finger. I thought I was going
crazy. I started laughing. I guess that was the point."

So, using a nail and a piece of scrap steel, and working for
two weeks, Stafford managed to drill a small hole through
the wall so he could talk to the man in the cell next door. He
also made a plug to fit in the hole for when the guards came
around. When the hole was finished, he and a man on the
other side, Ron Webb, used it to exchange jokes, as he had
done before with Ringsdorf. The hole was a convenience,
not a necessity. It was easier to talk than to tap.

One afternoon the man who was clearing was slow, and just as the signal shook the wall, the judas window came open and the guard caught Stafford and Webb cold. Both of them were at the wall, and the hole was unplugged. They were ordered out of their cells and up to the Big House for interrogation. Stafford and Webb were able to whisper back and forth on their way to the Big House, and get their story straight. They would explain to the interrogator that they were using the hole to tell a dirty joke — the truth and a good alibi since the Vietnamese were not likely to ask to hear the joke — and before it came to a head butting, they would agree to write letters of apology to the camp commander.

They were apprehensive as they crossed the porch of the Big House and went in through the doors. Nervous, but not panicky. They knew the routine, had been through it before, and it probably wouldn't be that bad.

By sheer coincidence, two POWs at the Zoo had chosen this time to attempt an escape that they had been preparing for more than a year. They had dyed their faces with iodine, put together outfits that resembled Vietnamese clothing, along with some improvised survival and signal gear, and come up with the outline of a plan. They left by way of a loose roof tile on a Saturday night when the guards were not alert. Several POWs watched through barred windows as the two men slipped across the yard and over the wall.

At daybreak they were hiding in a small stream behind some bushes. An old woman spotted them, and they were easily recaptured. They had gotten five miles from the camp.

Those two men were beaten and tortured with a renewed, almost desperate kind of savagery. One of them was never seen or heard from again. The Vietnamese later said that he had died from disease. The other man survived, remarkably.

In every camp the guards came tearing through the cells looking for contraband, and, inevitably, they found it. The offending POWs were beaten with strips of rubber, known as fan belts, thrown in irons, locked in solitary, and bent in the ropes.

In Plantation, Al Stafford and Ron Webb were already under interrogation. The first night was the usual — endless questions, sleep deprivation, the discomfort of sitting up straight on a stool for hours. Then, new interrogators appeared and everything changed. They were asked about their plans for escape and the names of the men on the camp escape committee. When they did not answer — because there was no answer, no plan, and no committee — the interrogators attacked. Stafford and Webb were beaten and then bent in the ropes. It was a while before they even heard about the escape attempt, so the sudden, unexplained fury of the Vietnamese made the torture that much worse, and it was as bad as anything since the Green Knobby Room. Webb's arm was broken. Stafford was beaten and bent until he heard his clavicle break. He made up an escape plan and told them that the head of the escape committee was a man who had been transferred to another camp a month earlier. Then he kept talking; revealed most of what he knew about the mailboxes, the camp chain of command, and anything else the Vietnamese asked for or might have been interested in. It went on for more than a month, in the interrogation rooms of the Big House, and before it was over, Stafford was trying to think of things he could tell them, anything to show that he was cooperating so they would throw him back in a cell somewhere and leave him alone, perhaps to die. He didn't care.

Finally, long after there was nothing left to tell, the Vietnamese decided either that there was no escape plan in place for Plantation or that Stafford had been used up. They were through with him. The interrogator told him, "Now you will go to a room alone and you will be alone forever." Threats were common enough and usually nothing more than threats. But this one had the ring of truth.

Stafford was led out of the Big House, across the yard, and around the warehouse. He could feel the eyes of the other POWs staring at him through cracks around doors and peepholes in the mortared-over windows. As he passed under his old cell, Warehouse One, where he knew Stratton would be watching, he signaled by drawing the flat of his hand back and forth across his neck — the sign for cutting someone's throat. It meant, "Cut me off." Stafford did not want to know the location of any new mailboxes, did not want to be included in the chain of command, did not want to be passed any new orders or information.

Communicating was too dangerous. The risk was not merely that you might be caught and tortured but, worse, that you might tell everything you knew. And giving away the location of a mailbox, or the camp chain of command, or anything else important to the resistance in Plantation made you feel worse than giving out nuclear bombing tactics or some information from the old days when you were in a squadron. The existence of a pitiful loose tile in the foul, stinking latrine seemed a more vital secret than anything you knew about nuclear bombs, and giving the location of that tile away, causing further pain to the other men in the camp, made you feel as if you had betrayed something more sacred than your oath.

But if you didn't know anything, then you couldn't give anything away. So as he walked down the line of cells, on his way to a separate shed where he would be the only prisoner, Stafford repeatedly drew the flat of his hand across his neck.

Cut me off.

The guard pushed him, almost gently, into his cell. It was one of three in a small block of cells at the end of the compound, near the latrine. The POWs called this little shed the Corncrib. Stafford was alone in his cell and the other two cells were empty. Which was fine with him.

The futile escape attempt had occurred on May 9, 1969. It was now mid-June. Not quite two years since Stafford had been shot down; since the morning when he woke up in the sweats of dread; since he had been blown — spectacularly and conclusively — out of the sky. He had been a prisoner now for almost two years, and the most likely prospect was that he would remain a prisoner a lot longer. He had been broken all the way down once. With help, he had bounced back. Now, he had been broken all the way down again. This time, bouncing back would be harder. He wasn't sure he had the will, and he didn't have the help. Didn't want it. Couldn't be trusted with it and didn't deserve it.

So he shuffled into his new cell and sagged onto the wooden bunk. When the guard closed the door and threw the bolt, he felt a kind of numb relief. He was alone.

Stafford remained alone, in the punishing heat, for a month. He spent the hours sitting on his bunk or on the floor, imagining that he was someone else, living a better life.

He was no longer figuring out solutions to sailing situations, trying to keep his mind tight on the problem. That required discipline. This was escape. He imagined that he was the director of the CIA and kept a tiger for a pet. He destroyed some of his enemies himself and set his tiger on the rest.

Sometimes, when he was not running the CIA, he was playing professional baseball. He had played the usual amount of baseball and other sports when he was a boy — maybe a little less, since he was one of those boys who cared more about hunting and fishing than team sports — but he had lost interest as he grew older. Some aviators followed sports passionately and could talk about them for hours. Others were indifferent, or bored by spectator sports, and would rather talk about cars, women, and airplanes. Stafford had been one of those.

But now, in the Corncrib, he played big league baseball. He made himself the pitcher, though he had never played the position or learned enough about it to know exactly what a slider was or how to throw one. So the games he played, in his feverish mind, did not have the rigor of his fantasies about sailing. When his team got into trouble, he would simply bear down and strike out the side. If his team needed a hit, he got it — more often than not a Promethean homer. The fans loved him. Especially the women and children. They filled his dreams.

There is one other fantasy he indulges during these days. It has no more discipline than the others, but it is more fully fleshed out and not so spectacular or heroic. If it isn't a disciplined fantasy, then at least it is realistic. It takes place in the realm of the possible.

He is a rancher. Owns a small spread just outside a town called Fairplay, Colorado. The name must have struck him sometime when he was studying maps and charts for a cross-country flight. He has never been there, but he is sure that it exists.

He owns a couple of cutting horses and runs just as many cows as he thinks smart. He grows some of his own feed and plants a vegetable garden. He cuts his own firewood, splits it with a maul, and stacks it by the cord. Every now and then he loads a few steers on a trailer and takes them into town for the weekly stock auction. He watches the mountaintops for the weather, and when he sees a storm coming, he makes preparations. He is capable and he doesn't need much. He gets by. He has neighbors, but he cannot see their homes and he does not miss having someone to talk to. He is self-sufficient and at peace.

Now and then the door to Stafford's cell would open and a guard would appear to escort him to the latrine to dump his bucket or to bathe. It was summer, stiflingly hot, and he was taken to bathe almost daily.

One day when the guard appeared, Stafford docilely reached for his bucket. The guard shook his head. So Stafford picked up his towel and bar of lye soap, but the guard shook his head again. With his index finger, he motioned for Stafford to follow like a timid child. They walked up to the Big House.

For once, Stafford felt no fear at all. In his mind it was late October in Fairplay. There was snow on the mountaintops and a chill in the air. He was on his way to a meeting of the Grange, not a quiz in the Big House.

When they reached the interrogation room and sat down at a table, he was shocked back to reality when he realized that the man on the other side was someone he knew. It was Doug Hegdahl.

The facts quickly established themselves.

"Al . . . Al . . . Al, are you all right?"

"Hi, Doug."

"Al, are you all right?"

This, it turned out, was the entire point of the meeting. Hegdahl had done everything that the Vietnamese required and was, at last, on the verge of being released with two other POWs, both officers and pilots. But at the eleventh hour Hegdahl had balked. "I'm not leaving until I've seen Al and know he is okay," he told the frustrated interrogators. Things were far enough along so that it would have been embarrassing not to release Seaman Douglas Hegdahl, as the waiting American delegation had been promised. So the Vietnamese decided one last time to indulge Heddle — the ignorant one, the peasant, the boy who had fallen off his ship. They brought Stafford to him.

"Al," Hegdahl said, "are you *sure* you're all right?" There was something about the way that Stafford looked at him . . . as though he saw him and recognized him and yet at the same time did not really know who he was. Or, worse, who either of them was. He looked, in other words, like a man who had lost his sanity. It had happened to at least one POW. That man had been taken away on a truck for "treatment" and was never seen again.

"Al, are you sure? Because I'm not going home until I know that you are okay."

Stafford had, by now, left Fairplay behind. He understood the situation with perfect, if temporary, clarity. He needed to convince Hegdahl that everything was all right so the kid would go home, like he was supposed to, and get those names out. He had to make sure that Hegdahl did not once again pull some last-minute grandstand stunt because of him.

"Fine, Doug. Everything is . . . just fine. Don't worry about me. You go on home."

Hegdahl looked at him skeptically. The guards were motioning for him to come with them, but he would not leave Stafford, who was now filled with a new kind of panic. This kid was going to blow it again. He would not leave this room *or* North Vietnam, and those names might never get back.

"Go home, Doug," Stafford said, trying to put a note of authority and command back into his depleted voice. "I mean it. I'm fine."

"Honest injun?" Hegdahl blurted, like a schoolboy.

It was a code, originally Dick Stratton's idea. He'd told Hegdahl to ask, "Honest injun?" when he did not know if an order given in front of the Vietnamese was meant seriously or not and could not be sure whether he should obey it or disregard it. If the answer came back, "Honest injun," then Hegdahl was to take the order at face value.

Stafford looked Hegdahl in the eye. "Honest injun, Doug. I'm okay. Go on home."

Sign and countersign. Hegdahl stood and nodded.

"God bless you, Al."

"God bless you, Doug."

Hegdahl left the room and, shortly after, was turned over to Rennie Davis, the antiwar activist, along with the two pilots. In a few days all three of them were back in the United States. Stafford was kept in the Big House overnight and interrogated about the meaning of the phrase "Honest injun," and also about the way he held his hand over his chest when he entered the room to meet Hegdahl. What was the code? they asked. What did the signal mean? Stafford had held his arm that way to ease the pain of his broken collarbone. He told them this and that "Honest injun" was simply American slang. They did not believe him and persisted. It was like that "Eat at the East End" T-shirt back in the Green Knobby Room, all over again.

Finally the interrogators gave up, and Stafford was returned to his cell in the Corncrib. On the walk across the yard he drifted back to Fairplay, where the snows were now falling in the valleys and it was time to get his cattle off to auction.

Once Doug Hegdahl was back in the United States and had visited with his parents and been extensively interviewed by intelligence specialists, he began meeting, almost immediately, with the wives and families of the men he'd known in

Plantation. Even while he was in the hospital he had been calling the families, and shortly after that the Pentagon sent him to meet formally with groups of wives, parents, and even the children of POWs he had known in Vietnam. The news he brought them was, in many cases, the first they had received. Barbara Hall, whose husband, Tom, was so good at improvising solutions to the POWs' housekeeping problems in Plantation, had not known for years whether he was dead or alive.

"I saw Tom," Hegdahl told her at a briefing in Norfolk, Virginia, "just before I left. He looked fine. A little underweight, but otherwise okay. And he told me to tell you he sends his love." It was like a gift.

When he had finished with the meetings arranged by the Pentagon, Hegdahl began traveling around the country, often by bus, to visit with the worried young wives and the parents of every man he had shared a cell with in Vietnam. He spent his own money on plane tickets and motel rooms. When he spoke with the wives and parents, he did all he could to reassure them, and he was careful not to cause them any unnecessary pain. But he tried to make sure that they understood just how bad conditions were in places like Plantation and just what the Americans there were going through. Many of the family members had grown frustrated by the government's efforts to spoon-feed them and placate them and generally treat them like a minor nuisance to be gently indulged. The Johnson administration — especially its first negotiator, Averell Harriman — had wanted to keep the POW issue out of the limelight and use quiet diplomacy to secure an accounting of the men and some improvement in their treatment. Hegdahl's reports helped these families in their resolve to force the issue and make it public. The Nixon administration bowed to the inevitable and made the POWs and their treatment and release a major theme. So much so it sometimes seemed that a primary objective of the war was to gain the release of a few hundred men who had been captured while waging it.

While the men who had been released with him did only as much as the Pentagon required — meeting in groups with families and talking extensively with the intelligence specialists — and then began putting distance between themselves and their experiences in North Vietnam, Doug Hegdahl kept a kind of faith with the men who had been his fellow prisoners in Plantation. This is the hard kernel of the Code of Conduct: I will keep faith with my fellow prisoners. His fidelity to the code and the simple decency he showed to the worried, desperate people he traveled around the country to visit made him a hero to them as well as to the men he had served with in Plantation. Women like Barbara Hall eventually distrusted everyone in the Pentagon, the State Department, and the White House because they told her very little and seemed so reluctant to do even that. But she believed, implicitly, anything the young sailor told her because he had been there and so plainly wanted to help. When he had done all that he felt he could do in the United States, Hegdahl went to Paris, where the negotiators were trying to arrive at a way to end the war. The trip was sponsored by H. Ross Perot, the Dallas millionaire who was highly active in the POW cause.

In Paris, Hegdahl lived for a while at the Hilton and then moved to cheaper, more agreeable quarters. At one point he visited the North Vietnamese embassy to discuss the POW situation. Evidently the Vietnamese did not remember him. He pressed for an opportunity to visit the camps, along with the Red Cross, and report on conditions there. The Vietnamese said that this was impossible but that they could assure him, and all who were concerned, that the POWs were receiving lenient and humane treatment. Hegdahl answered, "Maybe you don't understand. I know what kind of treatment they are receiving because I was *there*."

Hegdahl never did go back to Vietnam, but he had done more than Dick Stratton could have hoped when he ordered the young man to go home and tell his story to the world. He had gotten the names out to begin with. The Pentagon had not been sure whether some of the men whose names Hegdahl had memorized were alive or dead. Now it knew, and so did the families. Furthermore, before Hegdahl returned, the POWs had been forgotten by the government and the press as the larger, more visible issues of the war were endlessly covered and debated. His efforts helped make their status and treatment a continuing, major theme of negotiations and press coverage until the end of the war. To the POWs he remains a hero.

While Hegdahl was doing his work in the United States and in Paris, Al Stafford was sitting in his cell, drifting between the reality of the Corncrib and the tempting fantasies of Fairplay. Gradually he began spending less time in the mountains and more between the walls of his evil little cell. With time, he was healing and realizing that he had not been utterly broken.

Four or five months had passed since the escape attempt and the subsequent purge. He was pacing again and looking out at the yard to see what was going on instead of lying on his bunk, daydreaming about livestock auctions and pickup trucks.

But he was still alone, out of the resistance. There was no one on the wall he could tap to, and he did not know where the new mailboxes were located. He wasn't sure he wanted to know. Not yet, anyway.

He paced, worked fanatically at keeping his cell clean, and did memory drills as a kind of discipline. He made himself remember the names of everyone in his high school graduating class. Every teacher that he'd had in school. All of the women he had ever dated. He worked on gathering his mental and physical strength. He knew that he needed to be stronger before he could get back in the network.

In some fashion he was waiting for a sign. He could feel himself getting stronger, and there was no denying his hunger for some contact. But he could not quite make the first move, even though he thought about it almost obsessively.

Then, one morning as he stood at the door, watching through the cracks, he saw a POW on crutches being led slowly across the yard by a guard. The man had shockingly white hair, almost as though he had suffered some traumatizing fright. Stafford knew that the man had to be John McCain. Nobody else in the navy had hair like that.

McCain was the son and grandson of admirals. In fact, his father was commander of the Pacific Fleet. The Vietnamese knew this and had singled McCain out for special treatment, taking great satisfaction in extracting propaganda broadcasts from him. He had been filmed, heavily drugged, lying in a hospital bed recovering from his injuries a few hours after he was shot down and fished out of a lake in downtown Hanoi. He had been a special target of the interrogators ever since.

McCain had an uncommon ability to endure abuse and had bounced back from it again and again. He had become an inventive resister, one of the very best at screwing up the propaganda broadcasts. The other POWs considered him a master at garbling the syntax of the camp news.

As Stafford watched, McCain detoured out of his assigned path and hobbled a painful fifteen or twenty feet on his crutches before the guard could stop him. By then he was standing directly in front of Stafford's cell.

"Hey, Al, baby," he said, cheerfully, as though they were

meeting on the street somewhere. "You hang in there, now. Don't let the bastards grind you down."

Before Stafford could answer, McCain was gone, hauled off by the guard.

Stafford decided that it was time.

Getting back on the network was not difficult — just a matter of hand signals and coughing out messages in the tap code format. Within days he knew where the new mailboxes were. He began finding short messages when he went to bathe, and leaving a few as well, though he did not have anything of value to report, merely that he was all right.

One of the notes he found came from John McCain. It explained that he had been Stafford's replacement in VA-163 on the *Oriskany*, that he had also been through the Green Knobby Room, in a cell at Hoa Lo, and finally moved to Plantation, just like Stafford. The note ended with these words:

> Listen Al, since I seem to be following you around I would appreciate it if you didn't do anything stupid and get us both in real trouble.

Stafford was still in solitary and had begun to suspect that this would not change. The North Vietnamese seemed to focus on some prisoners and virtually ignore others once they had been interrogated and broken the first time after shootdown. As always, they followed no apparent pattern, except in the case of someone who had obvious propaganda value, like McCain or Robinson Risner, an air force colonel who had had the bad luck to appear on the cover of *Time* magazine not long before he was shot down, or one of the senior officers, like James Stockdale, who was the highest-ranking naval prisoner in North Vietnam. There was a grim kind of rationality in the way the Vietnamese bore down on them. But others, like Dick Stratton and Stafford himself, were simply middle-ranking pilots, virtually anonymous and interchangeable. There was no reason why the Vietnamese should single them out for special abuse.

When Stafford thought about this, the punch lines from two very old jokes occurred to him. The first was God's answer to Job's question, "Why me, God. Why *me?*" God answers in an eternally angry voice, "I don't know. Something about you just pisses me off."

The other punch line was, "I don't know. Just lucky, I guess." Stafford couldn't remember the joke that led up to the line. But the phrase itself was sufficient. It was part of the language shared by all military men.

"What do you mean, you can't go out tonight because you got the duty. You had the duty last weekend."

"That's right."

"Well, shit, how come you got it again?"

"I don't know. Just lucky, I guess."

Stafford had no idea why he was being left in what looked like permanent solitary. *Just lucky, I guess.*

But if he was going to spend the rest of the war in the Corncrib, that didn't mean he had to lie down and quit and spend the time daydreaming about ranches in the hills, pet tigers, and big league baseball. Once more he could feel himself bouncing back.

Twelve

IN SEPTEMBER the ruler of North Vietnam, Ho Chi Minh, died. He had been a mysterious man, a poet and a patriot, and many of the details of his life were never fully established. But there was no question that under his leadership the Vietnamese had beaten the French and won their independence as a nation in 1954. He was that rare thing — a communist dictator who was actually beloved by his people.

Stafford, of course, did not know that Ho Chi Minh had died. In his isolated cell he was not able to follow the news as it came in from new shootdowns or over the camp radio. When he stepped out of his cell for the walk to the latrine, the guard spoke to him, which was unusual.

"Stafford, this is time to be careful. Make no one angry."

"Okay," Stafford answered. It was the farthest thing from his mind. He had rallied, but not that much.

"President Ho Chi Minh has died," the guard said ponderously. "All the Vietnamese people are very sad."

"I understand," Stafford said, gravely. To himself he thought, *Romeo India Papa, son of a bitch.*

Some atonal, exceedingly melancholy music played over the camp speakers, and several of the guards, Stafford noticed, wept openly. The country, his escort went on, was in a state of national mourning. He did not have to add that a defiant POW would make a handy target for people feeling acutely nationalistic.

"Very sad," the guard said.

"Yes," Stafford said, "very sad."

Actually, Ho Chi Minh's death may have been the best news possible, short of an end to the war, at least from the POWs' perspective. Although the new leadership did not change broad policy on the war, some decision was plainly being made regarding the more than four hundred "war criminals" held in Plantation and other camps around North Vietnam. Almost immediately, living conditions in the camps began to improve. Brutal interrogations were not stopped, but they did become rarer, and the more sadistic guards and interrogators were transferred out of the camps — sent, the POWs devoutly hoped, to South Vietnam and the war.

The camp commander at Plantation was replaced, and the food got, if not actually *better*, then at least more varied and plentiful. And, most significant, prisoners like Stafford — men who had been in solitary or even in irons for weeks, months, and, in a few cases, years — were released from their terrible isolation and returned to the group, their fellow POWs, the men who had become family, squadron, service, and even country in their minds.

Some eight months after Ho's death, Stafford was let out of the Corncrib for the last time and returned to a room in the warehouse. When the guard opened the door to his new cell, Stafford saw two Americans standing by their bunks waiting to see who their new roommate would be. It was like that time, so long ago, when he had first been brought into Plantation in the middle of the night and escorted into the room with Parrott and Sawhill.

Stafford's new roommates were young and robust. They had been shot down later in the war than he and had not been broken as badly or as often. Also, he was senior to them, so they treated him with respect bordering on deference, as though he were not merely senior in rank but an elder of some sort as well. They included him in their conversations and in the games of catch they played with a baseball they had made from tightly wrapped rags. But there were times when he did not want to be included, and then they left him alone and did not try to persuade him to join in.

This was fine with Stafford. It was enough to be in a room with other men. He helped tap messages and he made decisions when he was asked. He talked a little and listened much more. He exercised and he paced, but without the old consuming energy. He had reached a point where he wanted, above all, to fade into the background, to become one of the herd. Bide his time, save his strength, hold on to his sanity, until someday . . . he would be sent home. From feeling as though he could prevail over his situation and dominate the conditions of his captivity, he had come to realize that he was severely limited in what he could do, *confined* in the worst sense of the word. He was learning the psychological tactics of passivity, an Oriental lesson.

His time in the cell with the two eager baseball players was short, about three months, during which nothing much happened. He had barely gotten to know the two when the guards came around and motioned for them to roll it up.

Stafford must have looked as stricken as he felt at the prospect of being all alone again, because as the guard was leaving the cell, he turned and said, "You will not be alone long. Only for two, maybe three days."

Stafford nodded and forced himself not to beg the guard to let him go wherever the others were going. Then he sat down on his bunk to wait, with a feeling of cold, wet dread filling his stomach like cement. If this was going to be the Corncrib again, then he was not sure he could stand it.

But the guard's word was good, and after a couple of tense days he returned. Stafford eagerly obeyed his instructions to roll it up, then followed him across the yard to a waiting truck. Several POWs were already sitting in the bed of the truck, holding their bedrolls. Stafford sat next to one of them.

"How you doing, Al?"

"Okay. Who are you?"

The man grinned as though he'd been waiting for this moment.

"I'm Ben Ringsdorf."

Stafford studied the man's face for a minute, then curled his hand so that his fingertips touched his palm. He looked through the small peephole his fingers formed. He'd never seen Ringsdorf any other way.

"Well, I'll be goddamned. You *are* Ben Ringsdorf. How's everything in Elba, Alabama?"

"Just fine."

"That's good. Real good. Now tell me, Ringer, have you heard any good feebles lately?"

The truck carried them out of Hanoi and into the countryside, where the peasants harvested rice and tended water buffalo in the ancient way. The men were not blindfolded, as they had been other times when they were moved around the country, and they studied the scene intently. It was entirely alien, although some of them had been in Vietnam now for almost six years.

After an hour's drive the truck arrived at a compound of small stone and stucco buildings. The men climbed down from the truck and looked around. The buildings were obviously new, and there were signs of hasty, just completed construction still littering the yard — good scrounging material. The camp was clean, and the POWs knew that with work, they could keep it that way. But there was a distressing message in all this. If the Vietnamese were using scarce resources to build camps for housing American POWs, then they were not planning on releasing them anytime soon.

Stafford, Ringsdorf, and a dozen other men were assigned to one of the huts. Once they were inside, Stafford and Ringsdorf unrolled their mats on adjacent bunks, almost automatically, and spent the rest of the day talking and catching up. After everything that had happened to him, and with the ominous significance of this new camp, Stafford took comfort in Ringsdorf's company. He was an old friend, a companion, and simply being around him made the load a lot easier to bear. Stafford found himself laughing again and racking his brain for some kind of pun to spring on Ringsdorf. They talked late into the night, long after the command to lower the nets and get under the covers.

In the new camp, under the regime that followed the death of Ho Chi Minh, the nature of resistance changed. Interrogations were not frequent and generally did not involve physical punishment or requests for propaganda or classified military information. They were manageable unless a man had flagrantly violated a camp rule or somehow provoked the Vietnamese.

But with the old tensions gone, boredom and a profound apathy became even more acute risks. The negotiations in Paris dragged inconclusively along while, in the South, the fighting and the withdrawals continued. There had been no bombing in the North for nearly two years.

The POWs knew enough, through the camp news, about all of this, and about the Nixon administration's strategy of "Vietnamization" — the plan to turn the fighting of the war over to South Vietnamese troops supplied by the United States — to realize that they might one day be the only U.S. servicemen left in all of Vietnam. To the Vietnamese, the POWs became more valuable as a negotiating stake with every battalion that left the South. More and more, they were hostages and not prisoners.

Jim Shively thought about this in detail. He had read extensively about the origins of the Vietnam War when he did postgraduate work in international relations at Georgetown. There was strong evidence, he thought, that the Vietnamese would not release the prisoners unless it were in exchange for something. They had behaved this way in the past, and there was no reason to think they would change now. Shively expected that if Vietnamization succeeded, then he might well be a POW for twenty years or more; that it could even be a life sentence for him and the other men in this camp. They became the most valuable chip the North Vietnamese had to bargain with.

Other POWs came to the same conclusion through intuition or from listening to Shively. It forced them to new conclusions about their situation. Active, immediate resistance had been its own implicit goal. You tried to frustrate the enemy and, in some psychological sense, defeat him. As long as you resisted, you did not have to question what you were doing. It was your duty, the part you played in the war. It was not flying supersonic fighters, but it was something. According to the code, your capture did not end your duty to resist; or, as the POWs often put it, a SAM may have separated your finger from the trigger, but you were still a combat pilot, fighting your country's wars.

But that implied a military war, with a logical, short-run conclusion. As the end of the war seemed more and more doubtful and the day of release receded farther and farther into the future, it became crucial to devise ways of simply living in captivity, of holding yourself together. It was as important to sustain yourself as it was to defy the enemy. The POWs had to make some kind of life out of very meager material.

The larger rooms in the new camp were an advantage in

the struggle against boredom and disillusionment. More men in a cell meant more conversation, more things to talk about, more skills to share. The greatest resource the POWs had was human talent, and they had never had as much of it as they could now gather in one place.

It was no longer necessary to tap each hand of bridge laboriously through a sequence of walls. Now the men played — with real cards from packages sent by families — for hours, forming partnerships, setting up tournaments, and establishing a system for awarding Hanoi master points. Exercise sessions were organized and records kept. And someone had the idea of forming a toastmasters' club, in which each man would speak for exactly five minutes on some topic. This led, inevitably, to educational programs. Now that Hegdahl had gone home, all of the POWs had had some college education. Most had undergraduate degrees, and some, like Jim Shively, had done postgraduate work.

So they began to teach one another what they knew.

Stafford, who had always been weak in math, asked for help from Charlie Plumb, the man who had tried to build a radio in Plantation, and an Air Force Academy man named Guy Gruters, who had gone to Purdue for graduate work in astrophysics. They tutored Stafford for hours, using the floor as a blackboard, until he understood the essentials of algebra for the first time in his life and could even work simultaneous equations, something that had baffled him all through flight training.

Euclidean geometry was popular, with its elaborate proofs. One man went farther and used a portion of the floor to work out the logarithmic tables. When a bad-tempered guard erased them, he simply started over.

Stafford had not been one of those boys who grew up with a passion for cars, teaching himself how to maintain and repair them, but he had always wanted to know more about engines. Now, in North Vietnam, it seemed the perfect time to learn. He wanted to be able to buy a pickup truck when he got home, an old stepsider like the one he had fantasized driving around his ranch in Fairplay. He wanted to be able to keep that truck running himself.

Tom Hall, the improviser, had a degree in mechanical engineering, and he knew cars. As a boy, he had strung chain hoists from tree limbs and pulled engines from cars and pickups, broken them down, replaced what did not work, and then put them back together. There was nothing mysterious about the internal-combustion engine to Tom Hall.

Also, he was one of the world's most agreeable men. When Stafford asked him questions about how valves and lifters work, Hall did his best to answer clearly, more eager to make himself understood than to demonstrate the breadth of his knowledge. When Stafford kept after him, confused but persistent, Hall finally said, "Al, if we're going to get into all this stuff, we probably ought to start right from the beginning and work on through to the end."

"Fine, Tom, long as you don't mind."

Hall looked around at the bare walls and wooden bunks. "No, Al," he said. "I don't believe I've got anything better to do."

Hall and Stafford spent hours talking about car engines, beginning with the essential operations and nomenclature and then moving on to practical trouble-shooting.

"Say she just won't turn over, Al. And you know the battery is good because you hear the starter motor cranking. Where do you start looking for the trouble?"

"I don't know. Gas?"

"Not bad. Let's say you know you have gas in the tank. What you need to figure out next is whether it is fire or fuel. So you pull the cap off one of the plugs . . ."

As Stafford and Hall worked their way through this ad

hoc course in automotive mechanics, they were joined by Joe Crecca, who also understood engines. Crecca was Italian, from New Jersey, and as hot-tempered as Hall was calm. Crecca was fierce in his loyalties, no matter how trivial, and one of his loyalties was to Chevrolets. He could keep other men's interest for days describing the way he had once put a Chevy V-8 into an Austin-Healey. Back in Plantation, the other POWs could always break the monotony by tapping through the wall to his cell with a message that read: PLS ASK CRECCA TO EXPLN WHY CHEVROLET IS NOT THE WORST PIECE OF IRON EVER TO HIT THE HIGHWAY.

Here, in the new camp, Crecca found an outlet for his considerable passion by helping Hall tutor Stafford in the fundamentals of automobile mechanics. From memory, Crecca drew detailed and complex schematics on cigarette wrappers, and Stafford began to feel with certainty that just as soon as he got home he could buy that stepsider, jerk the engine, and change the head gasket, just for openers. He imagined the garage full of tools and parts and the pleasure it would give him to know he didn't need some mechanic in order to stay mobile.

This "course," like others, helped pass the hours with less friction than the men had any right to expect, and the days seemed, at a minimum, not wasted.

Other men had other skills, which they began to teach in a somewhat organized fashion. Joe Milligan, a big man with a friendly, slightly sorrowful face and a sweet disposition, had grown up on a dairy farm in New Jersey, then gone on to agricultural school at Rutgers. He knew farming at both the practical and theoretical level. He was nicknamed "Hoss" because of his resemblance to the character in the TV series "Bonanza."

It is an abiding fantasy of many American men to someday quit it all for the country and a small working spread.

So Hoss Milligan began teaching a course in basic dairy farming, which expanded to include the fundamentals of biology and animal husbandry.

"Okay, Al," Milligan would say at the beginning of one of his lectures, "let's review what we learned yesterday. What are the five breeds of milk-producing cows?"

"Jersey, Guernsey . . ."

There was nothing idle or detached about the way the men studied their lessons. In some situations there is no room for ironic distance. It never occurred to them to step back and look at their situation. Here they were, halfway around the world from home, out of touch with their families, wearing pajamas, eating pumpkin soup, bowing to the men who held them captive. And how did they spend their time? Studying the internal-combustion engine and the fundamentals of dairy farming. They sweated over the lessons as they never had when they were bona fide college boys.

All around the camp, men kept busy teaching and learning, trying to recall the things they already knew or to learn things they thought they ought to know. Stafford diagramed sailing problems on the floor and explained them to an air force pilot who had never seen blue water except from the air.

"One more time, Al. What is the difference between a ketch and a yawl?"

In the evenings, the established off-duty forms of recreation continued: someone "told" a movie or a play. Stafford became known for telling the Broadway musicals that he had enjoyed so much. He would explain how he had taken a plane out for weekend cross-country hours and flown up to the field at the old Brooklyn Navy Yard and then stayed at the Edison Hotel near the theater district so he could catch *West Side Story* or *My Fair Lady*. Many of the men in his cell had not only never seen a Broadway play but had never been to New York, either. For their amusement, Stafford would describe his entire weekend, in every detail, including the women he had sometimes met in the city and taken out to dinner after the play.

The subject of women had become increasingly abstract for all of the men. It had been a long time. A few of the younger men were known to be technical virgins, inexperienced and, in these circumstances, no longer embarrassed about it. There were very few secrets among the POWs. These younger men often asked men who had been married for years what it was *like,* you know, living with a woman, the same woman, for Christ's sake, for a third of your life.

Conversations about sex were predictably coarse, at first, just like back in the squadron. But while that note never disappeared entirely, another became more prevalent. It had more to do with curiosity . . . longing. "Tell me about the way she was dressed when you picked her up at her apartment. Was she wearing perfume? Did she ask you up for a drink or something after you took her home? Did you *know* that she wanted you to spend the night?"

Inevitably, the men who were married thought about their wives. Some of them knew that their marriages had been in trouble even before they were shot down and probably would not survive after they got home. Everett Alvarez, the first pilot shot down in the war, learned in a letter from his mother, which the Vietnamese had opened and read, that his wife had divorced him on grounds of desertion and married another man. Others suspected that the same thing had happened to them and that they did not know for sure only because they weren't getting any mail. Almost always they were right.

"Wonder who the old bitch is partying with on my money tonight?" they would say. Others buried their worries as deep as they could, idealizing their wives to the point where they would not tolerate jokes and would take a swing at anyone who said anything out of line. Others, more secure, allowed just about anything in the way of banter.

"Hey, man, now that I know *exactly* how your old lady likes it served, I'm going to be at your back door every time you've got the duty."

"Well, just make sure you don't forget the baby oil."

"How could I forget?"

"And the ropes. You can't do anything without the ropes."

Al Stafford had been married to his second wife for less than six months before his squadron deployed. He had no good reason to think that she would be waiting for him when he got home. His first marriage had fallen apart under much less pressure. His wife was a good-looking young woman, and it was unrealistic to think that she would go into hiding and light a candle in the window every night until he returned. One thing he had learned since he was shot down, and that was to look at things plain.

But he joined the conversations about women, enjoyed them, actually, whether they were just low-down fighter pilot talk about sex or something more detached and abstract. He listened when some of the other men talked about how to make a marriage work. Fighter pilots generally let that part of their lives take care of itself. But they were going to be "playing catch-up," as one of them said. "In a whole new ball game," another added. They had heard enough now about miniskirts and the Pill and toplessness and the sexual revolution — things that were either unheard of or just breaking onto the scene when they had left home. Some of these men had missed fully half of the sixties. The seventies were already slipping by. Whenever they got back, they would be out of touch, relics of the past, men that time had left behind. Stafford wondered, if his marriage did break up or if it already had, whether it wouldn't be too late for him to try again, or if he would even want to. He planned, in the way the military does, for *contingencies*. The men would ask one another how they would handle various hypothetical situations. What would you do if you came home and found your wife had been living with another man but wanted you back? What if she'd had a child by that other man and, while the father was gone, she had kept the child? Would you be a father to the kid? What if your wife had divorced you but had not remarried? Would you try to go out with her and see if maybe she wanted to try again? They looked at all the variations they could imagine.

For Stafford, the most likely contingency seemed to be life as a bachelor fighter pilot (provided he could still fly when he got home). This life, he decided, would include a sports car and a sailboat. Also a truck like the one that he and Tom Hall and Joe Crecca worked over every day. His life would consist of rebuilding the truck, sailing the boat, and taking women out to dinner in the sports car. He would try to make that life work for him, if the old one, with the wife he had just been getting to know, went down in flames.

Jim Shively listened to Stafford talk about this bachelor life one night. When it was his turn, Shively said, "Well, that's fine, Al. But I'll tell you something. I went to an all-male college for four years. I lived in all-male barracks in flight school and when I got squadron duty. And now I have lived with nothing but men, here in beautiful North Vietnam, for just about five years. So when I get home, I am going to find some woman and marry her, and then we are going to have nothing but girl children. When I go into the bathroom, I want to see stockings hanging over the shower rod. When I wash a glass, I want to find lipstick on the rim. I want to see hairbrushes and hair curlers and bobby pins all around the house. I don't want to ever live with a bunch of goddamned loud, sweaty men again in my life." That became Shively's trademark line. Many men had one, and usually it began with, "When I get home . . ." The man would then go on to vow never to eat pumpkin, always to sleep with the lights off, to live where there were no mosquitoes, to eat off real china. Shively, who was not married, would live in a house full of women, surrounded by feminine things.

In some way this was at least part of what they all wanted. It was not just that they had been deprived of sex (and, when conditions were at their worst, of their sexual drive as well) but also that their world was unrelievedly, bleakly masculine in the worst sense of the word. Everything was hard, austere, and Spartan. This had its appeal to a military man. But these were also American officers who had grown up in suburban homes, gone to civilian schools and colleges, dated and married, raised families. For some, that domestic side of life could quickly become oppressive enough that it was a great relief to strap on an airplane and go off to bore some holes in the sky, or to sail off for a six-month deployment.

But none of them had ever been so entirely deprived of everything feminine and domestic for anywhere near the time they had already spent in North Vietnam. Even in conversation, they began to treat this other aspect of life with respect.

"Well, Jim," they would say to Shively, "I sure hope that you get just what you want. And you know what else? I hope you'll invite me to come stay with you now and then. I might not want to live like that, but I'd sure like to visit."

Thirteen

STAFFORD and the other POWs — some from Plantation and some from the Zoo — had been at the new camp, which they called Faith, for about four months, and had mentally dug in, when everything changed again, much as it had after the death of Ho Chi Minh. This time it was an American initiative that accounted for the change. A small group of volunteers from the U.S. Army Special Forces had attempted a rescue of the POWs held at another camp called Son Tay, less than twenty miles from Hanoi. It was an intricate, high-risk operation that had been in the planning and rehearsal stage for months before it was finally attempted late in November 1970.

The American troops flew from Thailand, across Laos and the waist of North Vietnam. They had to crash a helicopter into the middle of the prison compound since the space was not large enough to accommodate the blades. They were sheared off and the rescue force was on the ground almost simultaneously. The troops went from cell to cell, just as they had practiced, to free the POWs. It all went as smoothly as is possible for a military operation of this sort to go. But there was one terrible, overriding problem. There were no prisoners in the camp. They had been moved to another location because Son Tay was on low ground and tended to flood during the monsoon.

The rescue force got out as planned. There were no casualties — although one man was slightly injured jumping off the chopper — and they had killed and wounded a number of North Vietnamese troops (and possibly some Russian advisers) in a sharp firefight outside the prison compound. The raid was both a spectacular success, penetrating the heart of enemy country undetected and escaping with no losses, and a dismal failure. The mission — the rescue of American POWs — was not accomplished. Intelligence had, obviously, been disastrous. But the raiders had done their job with skill and bravery and were justifiably honored.

The raid was predictably controversial in the United States. It was seen as a provocation and a stunt by some, as a bold and necessary stroke by others. Typically, in this poisoned political climate some people seriously suggested that the Nixon administration and the Pentagon had known that there were no prisoners in Son Tay but had gone ahead with the raid in order to be seen as doing something and to galvanize their own supporters.

In North Vietnam the impact of the raid was immediate and dramatic. The POWs had reason to regret that it had failed — they could have been home by now — but the raid had done more to raise their morale than any other event in the preceding four or five years. It was a sign, the first, that they had not been abandoned by the government that had sent them here. And it was a strike, by God — action, for a change — and not just more discussions in Paris, appeals to world opinion, and quiet diplomacy.

The raid plainly rattled the North Vietnamese. This in itself was very satisfying to the POWs. The country immediately went on alert, as though a full-scale invasion might be next. Certainly a resumption of the air war was likely, or perhaps another, more determined attack aimed at freeing the POWs. In a way, these few hundred men had suddenly become the focus of the entire war, on both sides.

To defend the prisoners against a successful rescue, the North Vietnamese once again began moving them. Where they had once been dispersed around the country, in small camps, they were now concentrated, moved by truck from the various camps, into downtown Hanoi and the old French prison at Hoa Lo.

No clandestine raid would ever break the POWs out of Hoa Lo. The consolidation extinguished that hope. It also made a clear statement of just how highly the North Vietnamese prized their captives. They were not like the prisoners of most wars — an inconvenience for the side that held and was obliged to feed them, attend to their medical needs, and guard them. POWs were traditionally not much of an asset to their captors. But in this regard, as in so many others, the Vietnam War was different.

The morning after the Son Tay raid, the men in Faith were told to roll it up. The guards were no longer relaxed and casual. They yelled at the prisoners, pushed them, and stuck the muzzles of loaded AKs into their faces.

"Looks like no more Mr. Nice Guy," Ben Ringsdorf mumbled to Stafford as they sat next to each other on the ride to Hanoi and asked the inevitable question, "What is the significance of . . . ?"

When the truck had rolled into the big courtyard, the men were ordered out, lined up, and marched into a concrete room approximately the size of a basketball court. It was a vast space, by the standards the POWs had grown accustomed to, but then it was obvious that the Vietnamese intended to fill it up. By the time the big move was completed, there were more than fifty men in the one room. There were another seven rooms just like this one, and three smaller rooms, forming a triangle around a yard, and between thirty and fifty POWs were housed in each of these rooms.

There had never been so many POWs together in one place before. Almost as many were now in one of the eleven rooms as there had been in all of Plantation. The consolidation meant security for the North Vietnamese, but it also offered an unusual opportunity for the Americans. Numbers meant strength by way of organization.

For Stafford, coincidence made this new situation hard in a different way, one that not many other POWs ever experienced. While there was still some brutality in Hoa Lo — though nothing like what there had been back when the air war was going on — it was not torture but leadership that bore down on Stafford and a few other officers in each of what were known as the Big Rooms.

Someone in each room was senior — the SRO — and it was his job to organize the room, assign tasks, set policy, and, in general, assume command — the job that had fallen into Dick Stratton's lap back in Plantation.

At first Stafford was executive officer of his room in Hoa Lo — second in command, which was bad enough since the exec is by tradition the disciplinarian in any command structure. It is his job to "kick ass and take names," as they say in the military. But if that was a thankless job, at least the men understood that Stafford was not making the decisions or giving the orders, merely enforcing them.

But within a few weeks the senior man had gotten into a head butting with the guards over some trivial issue and was put in solitary.

"If I didn't know better, Al," Ringsdorf muttered, "I'd say he did it on purpose. Anything would be better than bossing this room. Al, baby, you have just grabbed hold of the bad end of the stick."

*

The command situation was as difficult as could be imagined, straining all the forms, patterns, and traditions of military leadership. The demands were harder under these circumstances; the rewards, the perks, meager to nonexistent. In the first place, military leadership generally works its way through a long chain of command, descending one rank at a time, until the men at the bottom of the chain and those at the top view each other from a distance, if at all. The commanding officer lives in separate quarters, generally more spacious and comfortable than those occupied by the men in his command. He is alone and aloof. He has aides and adjutants, and his remoteness makes the relationship easier on everyone.

But in Hoa Lo remoteness was impossible. Stafford slept nose to feet with the men in his command. Lacking a private office, when he needed to talk to someone alone, he used the latrine, a small, foul, walled-off space at one end of the room where conversations were kept short and to the point.

Complicating the lack of physical separation were rivalries and feuds that persisted however absurdly under the circumstances. Some POWs who had been in the Zoo and other camps considered Plantation a "country club" camp. This was an abiding distinction in the minds of men who remembered that the disastrous escape attempt had come from the Zoo while the early releases came from Plantation. They clung to this distinction, even though it was disparaged by men like Charlie Plumb, who had been shuttled back and forth between the two camps. But Stafford was a Plantation guy, and that worked against him.

Furthermore, he was not a graduate of one of the service academies, which even in these circumstances was a point of importance to some of the "ring knockers." Academy graduates resented taking orders from someone who was basically a college dropout and a cadet and had not been trained and groomed, as they had been, for flag rank.

Of course, some of the men in the room had become pilots only to avoid being drafted and serving as enlisted men. They were civilians in their own minds and barely tolerated military discipline, which seemed to them, under these circumstances, especially absurd.

Then there was the issue, among air force men, that Stafford was navy. Even under these circumstances the old interservice rivalry was still alive. Finally, Stafford's greatest obstacle was the fact that all the officers in his room were of middle rank — air force captains and navy lieutenants, for the most part — and many were junior to Stafford by only a matter of months or weeks. Stafford's position was not the result of some process of natural selection, some feeling that he was the one man for the job. It was a matter, almost, of bookkeeping: date of rank, a bureaucratic abstraction.

A man with only a few days' seniority could easily have taken command of a roomful of navy captains and commanders and air force colonels and lieutenant colonels. They would have been conditioned by a career in the military to defer to the SRO, and any other reaction would have been unthinkable.

But the men in Stafford's room were not so conditioned or so professional. They were still feisty, young, lower-ranking, and hard to control, even under the best stateside circumstances. Here they had been confined, starved, tortured, and degraded for as much as six years and never less than three. They were boiling over with hatred for their tormenters, desperate for some kind of release. If they could not be delivered from their enemies, then they would strike out in some other way. Even the best of Stafford's subordinates were bitter, frustrated, and demoralized. They were not happy about taking a lot of chicken-shit orders from someone who was no different, and no better than they were.

Merely organizing the room and assigning the men to the various details was tough enough. "Sweeping detail? Shit, I was on the sweeping detail yesterday. Why don't I get to clear for a change?" Pettiness was an alternative to self-pity, which was the last extreme.

While Stafford was in charge in his room, he received his orders from officers senior to him who were held in another part of the camp. All eleven rooms, and some four hundred men, had been organized as the Fourth Allied POW Air Wing, with Colonel John Flynn, the senior POW in all of North Vietnam, in command and Captain James Stockdale his deputy for naval affairs. Orders and policy directives came through the walls of their cell, to be dispersed through the Big Rooms of Hoa Lo as though they were separate bases or ships under some unified command getting their orders over the teletype, some of them highly classified and suitably encrypted.

Orders governing every conceivable subject came through the walls, or over them by means of hand signals, or now and then on pages of paper smuggled into new mailboxes. Many of the initial orders were modifications and restatements of the Code of Conduct. In large part these made Bounce Back the official policy for all POWs.

Then there were policy directives dealing with such matters as whether or not the POWs should stand when a guard entered the room (yes); whether they should bow to the guards (no); agree to read the camp news without first putting up some kind of resistance (yes, within limits); make public statements or confessions not extracted under duress (no); accept extra rations when men in other rooms were not getting the same food (no); and so forth.

These policy directives seemed to pour out of the room that held the senior officers. The men Stafford had assigned to communications were busy most of the time, listening, copying, and memorizing these directives, which were called Plums for reasons that no one has ever been able to discover. Inevitably, when a Plum came through the wall, some men would disagree with it, and Stafford would have to enforce the order. In one case he found himself ordering disgruntled men to stand up when the Vietnamese entered the room. The men stood but took their time about it, until Stafford had to shout, "Goddammit, get moving and get on your feet!" It made him feel like a fink for the Vietnamese, which was the point.

Some of the men, consequently, thought he was too soft. Others — men he'd lived with in Plantation — thought that he was too hard, that he had changed and turned on them now that he was in command. One day he had to give Tom Parrott the same order twice, and when Parrott began to complain, Stafford looked at him and said, "That's enough, *captain*. I gave you an order, now *get on it*."

"Aye, aye, *sir*," Parrott said, in a voice entirely different from the one that he'd used to tell his long stories about Dalton, Georgia, and explain why he always drove on General tires. From that day on, Parrott spoke to Stafford only when spoken to. The alienation of old friends was part of the price of leadership, and Stafford paid it with regret, and at a time when he could least afford it.

Men found all sorts of ways to express their resentment of the newly imposed discipline and chain of command. The signal and communications team worked incessantly, copying and relaying the Plums that came from the room occupied by the seniors. Command derived codes — simple transpositions and other more complex systems — to handle sensitive traffic. Instructions in how to manage various classifications using the codes were flashed by hand signals to Stafford's room from across the courtyard. Tom Hall was stationed on the concrete shelf that ran around the perimeter of the room and served as a common bunk at night. He would read off the message to another POW who memorized it then recited it to Stafford.

"Routine message traffic will be transmitted by routine

means," Hall said in a calm, laconic, farm-boy voice, as though he were describing the proper method for scalding a pig.

"Secret message traffic will be transmitted by secret means," Hall went on calmly. Then he looked down at the man who was memorizing the message and said, "Want to bet on what comes next?"

"Top secret message traffic," Hall said, "will be transmitted by top secret means."

The signaler from the other wall paused and then asked Hall to acknowledge receipt of the message.

He flashed back:

ROGER. MESSAGE COPIED. AND BULLSHIT BY ALL MEANS. OUT.

That response made it around the compound in minutes. The junior officers enjoyed it enormously, and the seniors sent out a couple of Plums regarding the sending of nonessential traffic over secure networks. But there were no punishments or reprimands. The senior officers at Hoa Lo were not without humor, and they were respected by the men they commanded even when the chicken shit got hard to take. Men like Stockdale and Risner had not simply shared the sufferings of the men they commanded, rare enough in modern war; they had also endured an extra measure of pain, torture, and isolation. The Vietnamese knew who they were and understood their importance to the resistance. They were repeatedly forced to make statements and sign confessions; and, inevitably, after the beatings stopped and the irons came off, they bounced back. Every man in the camps knew it, and that made it that much easier to follow their orders. While the junior officers bitched and griped, they also obeyed the Plums and stayed together, functioning as a unit and feeling the collective strength that comes from organization. The old military saw about a bitching sailor being a happy sailor seemed, in some strained sense, to hold true.

The men in what was now called Camp Unity had bounced back as a team.

Stockdale, Flynn, Risner, and the other senior officers in Hoa Lo raised the Bounce Back tactic to the level of an overriding principle to unite all the POWs now in Hoa Lo, even those who had crossed the line to become active, continuous collaborators with the enemy. Some of these men had been tortured into making statements and propaganda. Now they would do so merely if they were asked, and in some cases even seemed to volunteer.

The senior officers at Hoa Lo came up with a program they called BACK US, which was, in fact, an amnesty. Any man who had willingly collaborated was ordered to stop and to come back into the resistance. If he did so, there would be no questions asked and no recriminations, either in Vietnam or in the United States after the war, when they were all back home.

BACK US was the most extreme application of Bounce Back, and it worked as well as anything could have. Among the people who counted most, at the time when it mattered most, there were only two doubters, a marine lieutenant colonel and a navy commander who refused amnesty and continued making statements, meeting with delegations, accepting special treatment, and undermining the resistance to the point of trying to recruit other POWs.

They were unsuccessful. After the BACK US amnesty, the POWs in Hoa Lo remained remarkably unified and organized, despite the fact that they had been in captivity for years and had no good reason to believe that they would be freed anytime soon. Every man in Hoa Lo had all the justification he needed to say, "The hell with it," and make the best deal he could for himself. But only two did.

The price was paid in strained relations between the men taking orders and those in command. At one point those

strains became so severe that Stafford wondered if somebody else should take the job. He sent a message asking if
he should be relieved. The senior officers replied: NEGA-
TIVE. WE SUPPORT YOU AND THE JOB YOU ARE DOING.
Stafford's own supporters inside the room told him that
nobody could do any better and that they, at least, were with
him. He took a kind of solace from this and continued doing
what he could to run things smoothly and according to the
Plums.

It was probably hardest when he came into conflict with
one of the men he had come to rely on at Plantation, someone he thought of as a friend and comrade.

On one occasion some men were offered the opportunity
to write letters home and to have pictures taken to go with
the letters so that their families would be reassured about
their health. The rule was plain enough. Unless the opportunity was offered to everyone, no one could accept. No
special favors. There was no quicker way to drive a wedge
into the wall of unity the seniors were trying to build. Still,
men who had been in captivity for six years of a seven-year
marriage, who had children they had never seen, were desperate to get some message out to their families. It was an
irresistible offer, one that involved no outright betrayal of
their comrades, that did not help the enemy in any material
or even psychological way, that simply violated a rule that
made sense in the abstract but seemed pointless against the
need to get some word home.

Tom Hall, whose reputation as a resister and a loyal comrade was unassailable, was taken out of the Big Room for a
quiz and presented with this offer. When he returned, he
told Stafford about it and said he thought he would accept.
Stafford advised him against going through with the deal.
Hall listened respectfully. But he had spent three years in
captivity, during which time his family did not know if he

was dead or alive. He had not been allowed to write, while other POWs were and took advantage of their opportunities to do so. Hall had his picture taken and sent home to his family.

This was a clear-cut violation of one of the Plums, and Command immediately inquired if Stafford had given Hall a direct order. He replied that he had not. He was reprimanded, and Hall was stripped of his rank for a month — a purely symbolic punishment, but one that rankled just the same. One man in another cell sent word that when they got home, he was going to look Stafford up and "whip his ass."

So the price of unity was resentment, and a tension that found its release in ugly episodes. It was, no doubt, hardest on Stafford and other men in his position. But hard as it was, there was no question in the minds of virtually all of the POWs (especially *after* the war) that military training, organization, and discipline — chicken shit — was what saved them, in Hoa Lo and in the other camps, earlier in the war, when things were so much worse. Stafford often wished that someone else had been in command, that another man in the room had outranked him by a day or two, or that he had been able, somehow, to do a better job in an impossible situation. But he never wished for a situation in which no one was in command.

It was not always a happy band of brothers in Hoa Lo — how could it have been? — but it was never every man for himself, either. And unity paid off in some remarkable ways. The months at Hoa Lo, when the POWs were in the Big Rooms, turned out to be the best — or, more accurately, the least bad — of the entire ordeal. In an astonishing way, this was a remarkably productive time.

Fourteen

AT CAMP FAITH the POWs had learned that they could put something into the emptiness of the days by teaching one another the things that they knew. So they had improvised classes in animal husbandry and auto mechanics, and it had indeed helped the time pass. Now, here in Hoa Lo, they built on the lessons of this success.

Stafford appointed a man who'd had some experience in education as "dean of the college" and told him to find out who had the background to teach and in what subjects and then to organize a schedule of classes.

There was no shortage of men who knew enough to teach a course in *something*. Guy Gruters from Faith would continue his instruction in higher math. A man named Dave Luna, who grew up in Los Angeles, would teach Spanish. Another man, who had spent several tours with NATO, had learned enough to teach German. Jim Shively would teach international relations. Other men were qualified to teach history, psychology, American and English literature.

The dean of the college established schedules and assigned "classrooms." Some classes required larger amounts of space for blackboards, especially Guy Gruters' math course. His equations covered several square feet and ran wall to wall. Shively was able to get by on much less.

Classes began in the morning, after chow and cleanup, and ran all day. For the first time in the war, the POWs were able to write on something other than sheets of coarse toilet paper or cigarette wrappers. They were given small, lined composition notebooks and pencils or cheap pens, which they used to take notes. They would crowd in around their instructor at each of the classes and make their notes in small, economical script, hoarding the paper, which seemed infinitely precious. At night they would go over their notes from the day, memorizing formulas or dates or the definition of *watt, volt,* or *amp.* They were all schoolboys again, many of them studying harder than they ever had before. Joe Crecca taught a course in thermodynamics. The subject was beyond most of the POWs who took it, but Crecca was able to infuse the material with such passion that they called the course Thermo Goddammics.

As in any college, complaints about overwork, scheduling conflicts, and exams that came up on the same day were brought to the dean. Men struggling with difficult material would ask for extra tutoring. It was, in all the essential ways, a real school. Certainly learning was taken seriously, and the appetite for knowledge was great. There were no textbooks, however, and there was no library. All knowledge was held by the men who taught, and took, the course, which meant there was no source to which they could appeal when questions or disputes of fact arose. This was particularly hard on the men who taught the courses and who had not studied the material themselves for years. They were constantly being asked questions they could not answer or challenged on points of fact by someone who had also studied the subject.

These disputes were especially difficult. It was possible to teach around a gap in your own knowledge, but if a dispute arose, it had to be settled. These were the sort of men who were not temperamentally able to let a question remain in

doubt; they wanted to *know*, wanted it resolved one goddamned way or the other. "What I wouldn't do for one little
crummy set of encyclopedias and a ten-year-old almanac"
was a common refrain.

They improvised, as always. Often, a third party would be
called in to settle questions of fact. The communications net
could be used to find a man in another room with the credentials to settle the matter. WHAT IS ACTUAL DATE OF
BATTLE OF FUCKING WATERLOO would be tapped ur-
gently through the wall while a course in European history
waited for the answer. With five hundred men as a resource,
someone often did know the answer, could supply the missing information so that the course could proceed. But sometimes the men had to settle for what they came to call Hanoi
facts. Foreign-language idioms and the gender of nouns, especially, were settled by this technique. "Okay, men, we cannot establish for sure whether your French automobile is a
boy or a girl, but as long as we're here in Hanoi, it is going
to be a boy. When you get home and take your sweetie to
Paris, ask the concierge."

Instruction went on.

In addition to the academic basics there were electives,
and these turned out to be some of the best appreciated
courses taught in Hoa Lo. The subject matter was as eclectic
as the backgrounds of the men in captivity. One of the instructors, Jack Rollins, had begun his navy career as an enlisted man and had moonlighted to make some extra money
for his family. One of his jobs had been as a butcher. His
six-hour course in meat cutting was widely popular. Tom
Hall, who had always kept bees on the farm when he was
growing up, taught a course in beekeeping. Stafford taught
sailing, again. Men taught real estate, the stock market, and
cooking. Stafford's notebook contained, in addition to some
poems by Emily Dickinson, formulas for computing com-

pound interest, a detailed sketch of the human embryo, and a recipe for eggs Benedict.

You taught what you knew, even if you hadn't had any formal training yourself. Sometimes those were the best courses, the ones that came out of experience rather than the classroom. Thermodynamics and astrophysics were abstract brain teasers compared to a course in how to convert the garage of your house into a spare room. One man who had done it took his students through the entire process, step by step, from his pouring the foundation in a bad form so that it had to be broken out with a pick and started over, through ruining the sheetrock with the wrong nails, right down to starting the tile from the wall instead of from the center of the room. That he had made every possible mistake established his credentials in the most convincing way. Another man, teaching a course in diesel maintenance, told his students that when they removed an injector, they had to make sure not to let the crush washer fall down into the cylinder. It had happened to him, and he'd had to remove the head to get it out. Stafford made a careful note, since he was planning to buy a sailboat when he got home, one with a diesel engine that he would trouble-shoot himself.

Men taught courses in the most improbable subjects, even when they lacked the most fundamental teaching materials. A man who had been stationed in Europe and had done some amateur studies of the subject taught a course in wine appreciation. He instructed the men in the essentials of soil, sun, and vintages, and then told his students to imagine that they held a glass of some particular wine. "Now take a sip and notice," he would say, "that the taste is both dry and fruity." The men assembled around him would raise their imaginary glasses and taste the wine they had been discussing for the last hour. "I think you'll see why this is a particularly good wine to serve with game."

Men made notes to buy the wine when they got home.

Joe Crecca had grown up listening to classical music the way other men had listened to show tunes or top forty. His parents had taught him, by example, to love the music, and he had learned, on his own, about the lives of the great composers and the stories behind their most famous pieces. So he taught a course at night, after the normal workday was finished, in classical music. With all his considerable enthusiasm, he would hum or whistle the opening bars of some immortal symphony and then launch into a passionate account of the life of the man who had composed it. One night he was discussing the life of Mozart. By the time he had reached the composer's poverty, early death, and burial in a pauper's grave, he was in tears.

Another man had enough background in choral music to form and direct a glee club. It practiced every night and then, on Sundays, sang hymns at the regular church services. Men who had no use for church would gather at the appropriate end of the Big Room to listen to the hymns. Afterward they'd say, "You know, the guys in that goddamned glee club sounded really *good*."

In all this activity there was release and purpose, a way to fight off the slow slide into apathy. Everyone wondered just how long the war would go on and how long he could continue. Some men kept saying six months, and a few had begun to let themselves believe forever. Mike Burns, one of the younger men in Hoa Lo, had been shot down when he was twenty-two, in the summer after Johnson had suspended bombing above the twentieth parallel but before he ordered all bombing of North Vietnam halted. Burns was on his eighteenth mission when he went down, had been "in country" for only a month. He was from a blue-collar neighborhood in Indiana and had learned to fly while he was in ROTC in college. Now he was here, in the Big Room at Hoa

Lo. He had been in North Vietnam for almost four years, longer than any American pilot had been held by the Germans in World War II. Captivity was the dominant experience in his life.

Burns was one of the quiet ones, who did his part and made things easier on everyone else. Stafford counted on his support when he had trouble getting other men to obey his orders and abide by his decisions. After he was shot down, Burns had nursed a couple of other pilots who were seriously injured all the way to Hanoi and continued caring for them for months after that in an isolated cell in Hoa Lo before he was moved out to Plantation, then Faith, and finally back to Hoa Lo. Because he was younger and more inexperienced than most of the other men, he would ask for advice, listen, and keep his own counsel.

He talked to Jim Shively a lot because Shively seemed to know things, and when he did not know something, he did not act as though he did. Burns talked to Shively about the war and his theories about Vietnamization. He was persuaded by Shively's arguments that successful Vietnamization of the war amounted to a life sentence for the POWs. Shively's arguments were intellectual and analytical. Other men came to the same conclusion viscerally. They told Burns to face the fact that they were expendable. Burns hated that word.

But he decided it was only prudent to think that Shively was right and to begin living as though he would be in Hoa Lo for twenty years. He was determined to go home someday, and the way to make sure that he would was to think in those terms. Not six months, not according to the latest rumors about progress in Paris, not according to the significance of some minor change in camp routine, but according to the hard logic of the situation. Twenty years. He would still be in his forties when he got home, and when that day came, he did not want to come out a wasted old man, some kind of pathetic parody of Rip Van Winkle. He would have a world of catching up to do, but at least he would learn what he could while he was here, keep his mind as sharp as possible and his body fit. He could avoid getting either too high or too low. He could make it the point of his life to maximize whatever resources he had available.

So he took all the courses he could manage. He had never drunk wine, but he took the wine appreciation course and memorized the vintages that he thought he would like to drink when he got home. He took Crecca's course in classical music and learned the opening chords of as many pieces as he could and everything that Crecca taught about the lives of the composers. He had grown up in the Midwest, but he learned the principles of sailing and navigation, the rules of the road, and all the other things that Al Stafford taught in his course. He memorized Shakespearean sonnets and the details of the battle of Thermopylae. He sang in the glee club.

One evening, after a day full of all this activity, Shively and Burns were talking quietly in the thin, gloomy light of the large cell. Card games were starting up around the room, and other men were gathered in small groups to listen as someone "told" a movie. It was the end of another day in captivity, another day that anyone who had not lived it would have called wasted. Given the choice, not one man in the room would have chosen to be there.

"You know," Shively said in a soft, ruminative voice, "I think everybody ought to do this. Not for as long as we've had to do it. But maybe for a year."

Burns wasn't sure, but he thought he understood what Shively was talking about. And he was sure that most of the other men wouldn't — would think, in fact, he was crazy.

*

For Al Stafford, the pressures of command eased with time and the support of several loyal men who more or less became his staff. His executive officer, a large marine pilot named Jerry Marvel, helped enforce unpopular orders and was imposing enough when he passed the word that few men argued with him.

The POWs called their compound at Hoa Lo Camp Unity, and that spirit prevailed, despite all the small, inevitable frictions. On the POWs' first Christmas in Unity there was a celebration of sorts. Marvel managed to approximate a Santa Claus costume. Three men dressed up in rags made to look like women's clothing and performed a skit in which three virgins were sacrificed to a volcano, which threw them back. Other men did the old belly whistling gag.

Every man in the room had put his name on a piece of paper, and then they had all drawn a name from the pile. Each man then gave a gift to the man whose name he had drawn, just as if they were back in school somewhere. The handicap was, of course, that they had nothing to give. They got around this problem by imagining what they *would* give if they were back home and had access to the stores and PXs of their other life. The rule was that you had to be realistic — you couldn't give someone a mansion full of beautiful, willing women — and you had to try to make the gift something that was appropriate for the man receiving it.

So men gave one another fly rods they remembered hearing them talk about fondly or a set of particularly good hand tools. The man who drew Stafford's name knew that he enjoyed reading naval history, so he gave him a set of Samuel Eliot Morison's books about the U.S. Navy in World War II. Stafford gave the man whose name he had drawn a set of Stan Getz albums because he liked jazz.

After the presents were opened, the glee club performed, and then all the men sang. They sang the usual hymns, including "Silent Night," which filled them with all the sweet and melancholy feelings that song evokes. But the hymn was touched with another note, a profounder sadness and deeper longing than Stafford could ever remember feeling. He recalled the stories he'd read of German and English troops leaving their trenches on the first Christmas of World War I and mingling in no man's land, where they sang that hymn, first in English and then in German. For a few moments he felt a sense of peace.

◼══◼══◼

Fifteen

THE NEGOTIATORS in Paris were having a harder time
finding a formula for peace. They met both in open
sessions that were more or less for show and also in
secret — Henry Kissinger and Le Duc Tho each making his
government's case, unhampered by public scrutiny — but the
war went on. The North Vietnamese launched a conventional invasion of South Vietnam; the Nixon administration
responded with heavy air support for the South Vietnamese
army and by mining the port of Haiphong. It was an esca-
lation that had been urged by the military for years. Air
raids were also conducted on Hanoi, and these led to an
international outcry. But neither the protests nor increased
military action seemed to break the stalemate — or free the
prisoners in Hoa Lo.

They did produce some new POWs, who brought in news
from the outside. Their untainted reports, combined with
the slanted news the men in Hanoi were getting from their
captors, helped them form a picture of what was happening
in the world outside. It was an election year in the United
States. Nixon was running for reelection against George
McGovern. The POWs held their own mock election, and
Nixon won even more decisively than he did in the actual
vote back home. McGovern received a half-dozen votes or

so, including those of Jim Shively and Mike Burns, who were convinced that the more Nixon's program succeeded, the bleaker their outlook became.

In spite of the unity and the strong organization within Hoa Lo, some of the men grew increasingly demoralized. One good resister told a senior officer, "Look, I'll hang in there for another year, but that's it. If I'm still here then, I'll make any deal I can to get home." He had been in North Vietnam for over six years.

For Al Stafford, who had been in captivity almost five years when the port of Haiphong was mined and U.S. planes began attacking the same bridges that he had been shot down trying to take out — this time with laser-guided "smart bombs" — the end seemed both near and still very far away. With the help of Marvel, Shively, Burns, Ringsdorf, and other men who backed his leadership, he had gotten a handle on the organization in his room. There were still episodes of resistance and resentment but no more talk, from him or anyone else, about his being relieved. On July 4, 1972, the POWs celebrated with skits, songs, and speeches. Stafford was the last to speak, since he was in command. He recited the words to "America the Beautiful" with as much force and conviction as he could manage.

"I think we all need to think about those words," he said, his voice thick with emotion. "And we need to remember those words when we lose patience, start bitching and bickering among ourselves, and forget who we are and why we are here. We are still American fighting men, trying to do a job for the land that we love. We need to remember that, and we need to help each other through the hard times."

When he finished the speech, he felt that he had made an impression, even on the men who had not supported him. All fifty men in the room cheered, and when he stepped down off the slab that was their common bunk, they reached out to shake his hand and pound him on the back and shoulders. They were all still patriots in that room, but Stafford — and probably most of the others — wondered how much longer it would be before that reservoir ran dry.

Stafford had begun to keep notes as a way of making his own tangled feelings clear to himself. On the back of a cigarette wrapper he copied lines from one of the few books that had somehow made it into Hoa Lo, sent by families in the United States in packages that were intercepted and partially plundered.

> Your life and your death are nothing to these fields — nothing, no more than it is to the man planning the next attack at G.H.Q. You are not even a pawn. Your death will not prevent future wars, will not make the world safe for your children. Your death means no more than if you had died in your bed, full of years and respectability, having begotten a tribe of young. Yet by your courage in tribulations, by your cheerfulness before the dirty services of this world, you have won the love of those who have watched you. All we remember is your living face, and that we loved you for being of our clay and our spirit.

The passage was from a memoir called *A Passionate Prodigality* by Guy Chapman, who had been a British infantry officer on the Western Front in World War I. The lines struck a deep chord in Stafford and many of the others in Hoa Lo. The words went beyond the blunders and the oratory of statesmen; beyond any of the abstractions about the war. In this brief passage was the reality of their imprisonment and their loyalty to one another.

Two weeks after the July Fourth party, the U.S. Senate passed an amendment to a bill prescribing total U.S. troop withdrawal from Vietnam, contingent on the release of the

POWs. Their fate was now an issue in the election. Nixon supporters charged that McGovern would end the war without any assurances that the POWs would be returned. McGovern and his backers answered that as long as the war continued, there was no chance the POWs would be coming home.

Not long after the celebration, Stafford once more rolled it up. The Vietnamese moved some two hundred men, almost half the POW population of Hoa Lo, across town to the Zoo. They remained there for a month and then were moved again by truck, this time deep into the countryside, north, almost all the way to the border with China. Their destination was an old prison compound in a remote agricultural valley untouched by the war, or by most of the twentieth century for that matter. The POWs called the compound Dogpatch.

It was impossible to know the reason behind the move, but some of the men believed that the Vietnamese were hoarding their assets. If the war ended in some tangled cease-fire and prisoner exchange, the North Vietnamese would hand over the men left behind at Hoa Lo while, up here in the boondocks, they would hold on to the men who remained for use as ransom in future deals. Tensions in the war were rising; so were the prospects for peace. Just about anything seemed possible.

So the men in Dogpatch either played the old game of "What is the significance of . . ." or, like Mike Burns, ignored speculation, rumor, and even hard news, concentrating instead on keeping their own counsel and tending to their own needs. In Dogpatch the POWs were given more freedom than they'd ever experienced before in North Vietnam. The rule against communicating was lifted. Within the several small stone huts that served as cells, the men talked, conducted courses, exercised, read the few available books over and over — anything to break the monotony. Some even tried to make moonshine. They used pears for the mash and managed to achieve fermentation, but the container — a brand-new bucket that had not yet been used as a toilet — was made of iron with a zinc coating which was eaten away by the alcohol. Those who drank the unappealing brew suffered some mild poisoning. That was as close as life in the Vietnam POW camps ever came to "Hogan's Heroes," the popular television show back home which depicted life in a World War II POW camp as resembling a series of college-boy escapades and pranks.

Late in October 1972, as it was turning cold in the mountains and the monsoon was gathering, Henry Kissinger announced, "We believe peace is at hand." Stafford told himself not to get excited. He had heard it all before, and besides, there was no guarantee that any deal would include him.

Nixon was reelected, and for a month and more after that no peace treaty was signed. The statesmen had come close but could not conclude their negotiations. A week before Christmas the POWs who were still in Hoa Lo were awakened in the middle of the night by waves of B-52 bombers flying high over the city. They watched as SAMs cut glowing arcs through the night and, once or twice, hit their targets; the exploding bombers lit up the sky. The bombs fell in patterns that were half a mile wide and two or three times that long. The city burned and the walls of the old prison trembled. Inside, men cheered and the guards did not try to quiet them.

It went on for a week. The big bombers came at night, the smaller planes during daylight. The city was under attack almost constantly until Christmas, which was quiet. But the attacks resumed the next day, lasting for eleven days altogether.

The Christmas bombings, as they came to be called, remain controversial — pointless and barbaric according to one view, necessary and overdue by another. Among the POWs, then and much later, the feeling was that the bombing ensured that they would all go home once the peace papers were signed. Before the bombings they had been hostages and represented an asset of sorts. But if the POWs could be used as a pretext for military action — for more B-52 raids — then they were not worth any possible ransom. Jim Shively and Mike Burns, who had been so pessimistic about their prospects if Vietnamization succeeded, believed that without the Christmas raids they might have spent another fifteen or twenty years in Hanoi. Neither they, nor the Vietnamese, had counted on anything so dramatic or violent, especially not so late in the war.

Stafford and the other men in Dogpatch knew nothing about any of this. They had not been told about the Christmas raids or about the signing of the treaty on January 27. They celebrated the new year — 1973 — and did their best to keep warm and occupied. Then, one night, the guards called them out of their huts and began putting them in formation according to some new system. A man's name would be read out from a sheet of paper, and he would be assigned a place. It was like the first day in some new command, or at boot camp, except that there was no apparent rationale for the way the ranks were formed.

Tom Hall was the first to figure it out.

"Hey, you know what," he said, "they're lining us up in order of shootdown. This time I believe we are going home."

The other men quickly looked over the formation and checked it against what they knew about shootdown dates — and they knew a lot. Hall was right. They *were* being formed according to how long they had been in captivity. If there was any significance at all in that, then it could mean only one thing.

Some men cheered. Others, like Stafford, were mute. It had been so long, and they had been burned before, many times. When the reorganization was complete, and the men were in their huts according to this new grouping, some talked excitedly, certain that this was it. Others kept to themselves, refusing to allow themselves the luxury of hope until they were actually on their way out of Vietnam. No one slept.

A few days later they rolled it up again. The optimists believed that this was the last time. The others went about it mechanically. The trucks left Dogpatch for the long ride back to Hanoi. At the end of the line, Stafford found himself back at Plantation.

It was the last place on earth he would have chosen. He imagined the worst: a return to the way things had been back before Ho Chi Minh died, before the raid at Son Tay, the move to Unity. He felt the helplessness and the rage of someone who is being toyed with, like a mouse tormented by a cat before the kill. At one moment release seemed logical and imminent. Then, the next thing he knew, Stafford was back at the scene of his worst moments in Vietnam, the worst time of his whole life. As he climbed down from the truck, he looked at the Corncrib the way a man on death row might study the electric chair.

But the guards did not push, shout, or order the POWs not to talk. They merely pointed the men toward the cells, where they unrolled their mats and stored their things. Then, since the doors were still open, they left the cells for the freedom of the yard, where they mingled and talked like schoolkids at recess. They might be back at Plantation, but it was not 1969 again.

At lights out the men were sent back to their cells, and the guards came around to lock them in. It was the first and only prisonlike gesture of the day. Still, Stafford felt the old claustrophobia returning, and he paced for an hour or two before he could lie down on his board, cover up, and sleep.

The prisoners had been at Plantation for only two or three days when they were called out into formation. There was the usual mumbling of men trying to guess what was up. After a few minutes the guards began handing each man a few sheets of mimeographed paper. These were copies of the Paris peace accords. It had been an American condition that each POW would receive his own individual copy and that the treaty would be read to them.

For many of them, even seeing the words on paper was not enough. "I'll believe it when I'm on the plane and feel the gear retracted," one of them said. "Feet wet and I'll know I'm going home." For others, it was now a sure thing.

Stafford was one of these. But for some reason he did not feel anything. Not the elation, the boundless joy he would have predicted feeling at any point in the last five years. Not even the kind of physical release, in the form of laughter or tears, that would have seemed inevitable to anyone imagining himself in the same position. As he read the dry language of Henry Kissinger and Le Duc Tho, for which they would receive a joint Nobel Peace Prize, what Stafford felt was a kind of emptiness which changed, slowly, to profound, bottomless fatigue. He had never felt so tired, and so vacant, in his life. He wanted, more than anything else, to go back to his cell, lie down, and sleep.

According to the agreements the POWs were to be released in four groups. Sick and wounded first, with the remaining prisoners going home according to shootdown date. The cease-fire had taken effect on January 27, 1973. Two weeks later, 116 American prisoners were flown from Gia Lam Air Base in Hanoi to Clark Air Force Base in the Philippines. The first man off the plane was Jeremiah Denton, who had been shot down on July 18, 1965. It was Denton who had blinked his eyes to spell out the word *torture* in Morse code during a propaganda film. He had been one of the strongest resisters and would later receive the Congressional Medal of Honor for his actions while in captivity. He spoke for the waiting television cameras and microphones:

"We are honored to have had the opportunity to serve our country under difficult circumstances. We are profoundly grateful to our commander in chief and to our nation for this day."

Denton paused. Those were the words he had rehearsed on the flight over the Pacific. The crowd seemed to expect something more, so he concluded with the first words that came to mind.

"God bless America."

While the first group of POWs were being cheered, debriefed, and reunited with their families, the remaining men waited in Hanoi, where things went along the way they always had during this confusing, frequently absurd war. When Henry Kissinger flew into Hanoi, the Vietnamese decided to release twenty POWs to his custody as a gesture of friendship. These men were selected out of shootdown order, on an ad hoc basis, and their first response was to refuse. Eventually a senior officer with the Kissinger mission had to order them to "get your asses onto that plane." Those were considered "competent orders," and the men left.

The second group of POWs scheduled for release were assembled and fed a farewell meal of freshly killed duck, eggs, and beer. But the release did not occur as scheduled. The men went back to their cells and a new form of torture.

Three days later they were given another farewell meal. This time they boarded the waiting air force planes and left Vietnam.

Stafford's date of shootdown was late enough in the war that he just missed the cutoff for this group. He would be part of the third contingent to leave, in mid-March. Oddly, he was in no hurry. After five and a half years, a few more days, one way or the other, did not make that much difference. Besides, he was in the grip of an abiding apathy. Everything now seemed so inconclusive — to be wrapped up like this, in the usual bumbling bureaucratic fashion, after all that had happened. He did not know what he had expected — to die, perhaps, in Vietnam — but he knew that he hadn't expected it to end this way. He remembered the line of poetry about how the world will end "not with a bang but a whimper." That seemed about right.

He thought about what he would find when he got home, how he would be received and what his life would be like. Perhaps because he had learned to see things absolutely straight and without sentimentality or false hope, he understood that it would not all be easy or painless. He wrote his thoughts about homecoming on a cigarette wrapper:

Release could be a dangerous and traumatic period. People are not as sympathetic as you expect. Loved ones may be dead or no longer love you. You were acutely alive to yourself all those years, but partly dead to them. They lived in your mind, from your memory of them. Such a memory is static. They lived all that time in a dynamic, changing world. You may resent changes in them that you would not have even detected had you been there to change with them. Your years of trial and soul-searing emotional agony in prison may not end with mere release. The first days and weeks of rehabilitation can be fraught with danger too. Have faith. Once this trial is over, all of it . . . the years in prison and the disillusionments of return, you will be able to regard it as one big nightmare and then press on with life. Carry with you that nothing will be that bad again.

Most of the men around him were eager, almost cheerful. One of them, a man who had known Stafford for a while and had helped him through some of the difficult times in the Big Room, saw Stafford sitting alone one day and took a seat next to him. "Hey, babe," he said, "how's it going?"

"Good," Stafford said, automatically and without conviction.

"Uh huh."

"How about with you?" Stafford said.

"I'm okay. I won't be 'good' until I'm at thirty thousand feet, flying zero niner zero away from this place. But I'm okay. Listen, Al . . ."

"Yeah?"

"You've got to pull out of it, man. You don't want to go home like this. No matter how you feel. You know what I mean?"

"Yeah. I do."

"I know you can't help how you feel, but listen . . . the hell with how you feel. Make like you feel great. Just fake it till you make it. You're going home, man. Out of this place. You can't let them — or anyone else — rain shit on that parade."

"I know," Stafford said.

"Is there anything I can do?"

Stafford shook his head. "No. Thanks. I don't even know what the problem is."

They talked for a while, about what they would do when they got home. The plans were less extravagant than they had been back when going home seemed to be something they might not live to experience. Stafford talked about buying an old pickup, tearing it down, and rebuilding it. Thinking about that had kept him diverted for hundreds of hours while he was here, and he believed it would make him happy when he was back home. He did not know how he would be received by the navy or by his wife. Did not know where he would live or what kind of work he would be doing, whether he would be a married man or a bachelor. But however it worked out, he could have that truck and work on it the way Crecca and Hall had taught him. For some reason that seemed important, and the other man seemed to understand completely.

On the day before they were scheduled to fly home, Stafford and the others were issued some clothes to replace their prison pajamas: work shirts and pants, cotton windbreakers — the sort of clothes a parking attendant might wear. They were also given a pair of plain black leather shoes to replace their rubber tire sandals. The shoes pinched Stafford's feet badly, and he was sure they were the wrong size. But it was simply that he was not accustomed to wearing shoes. The final item of new gear was a small gym bag to hold any personal effects a prisoner might want to carry home. Stafford packed the notebooks he had filled, along with his tin drinking cup and the faded pajama tops he had worn for so many days and mended hundreds of times with improvised needles.

On the morning of their scheduled release, the men were fed breakfast and then loaded onto buses and driven across Hanoi to the airport. There, they saw the big air force C-141s waiting, with their cargo ramps lowered, to take them aboard. American military men and even some women, in uniform, stood at the large, dark entrances to the planes, talking and smoking while they waited for things to get moving. It was a scene that might have been played at any base where they had ever served.

The POWs got off the buses, formed ranks, and were marched over to tables manned by officers from North

Vietnam and the United States. As each man's name was read off a roster, he stepped forward. The Vietnamese put a check by his name on their roster, and the Americans did the same. Custody had changed hands.

When Stafford's name was read, he stepped forward and saluted the American officer in charge. He was directed to one of the large transports and walked across the concrete apron and then up the steel tailgate, where he was welcomed by an army nurse who showed him to a seat on the plane and asked him if he had any immediate medical problems that needed attention. He said no.

Then how about a cup of real coffee, she offered.

That would be great, he said.

It took an hour, perhaps, to complete the transfer. When the paperwork and other formalities had been concluded, the cargo ramps were raised into place, sealing the planes, and the engines were brought up to full power. One by one, the big planes taxied out onto the twelve-thousand-foot runway and took off. Stafford felt as if he were holding his breath while the plane built up speed. Then the wheels left the ground and were retracted. He could see the coast and the Gulf of Tonkin, just the way it had appeared five and a half years earlier on the morning when he woke up in the grip of that bad feeling. Under the wing he could see the target of that day's attack and the SAM site that had launched the missile that blew him out of the sky. He felt, at that moment, that he had somehow accomplished his mission at last.

As the big plane crossed the coastline and there was nothing but water below, someone shouted, "Feet wet, baby. We made it." Stafford felt as though some constriction had been cut away within his chest and he could breathe again. He and all the men around him began cheering, laughing, and pounding on one another with unrestrained joy. They were free.

Sixteen

A BAND WAS PLAYING, flags were flying, and cheering crowds were waiting when the big transports lowered their ramps and the POWs stepped down onto the tarmac at Clark Air Force Base. They had all wondered, at times, just how they would be received when, and if, they ever got back home, and this reception was an answer of sorts. During some of the worst times, when the men had been forced to make statements and meet delegations, they had imagined that they would be met by officers with briefcases and hard faces, who would read them the articles of court-martial and warn them of their rights.

The ceremony was brief but reassuring. As the newly free men stood in the sunlight and listened to the words of welcome, the cheers, and the brisk martial music, the first, most dreadful layer of uncertainty fell away. It was as though they were heroes, even if Stafford and the others did not see themselves that way, any more than they considered themselves collaborators. They felt they had done the best they could. No more nor less.

From the airstrip it was a short ride to the hospital, where medical teams were waiting. At the door Stafford was met by a nurse, a medic, a doctor, and, for reasons that he did not understand but considered ominous, a chaplain. The medic pointed the way down a long, tiled corridor, and they began walking. No one said much for the first hundred feet. The chaplain walked three or four paces to the rear, and Stafford assumed that the clergyman had bad news from home — a death in the family — and that he was waiting for a chance to get Stafford alone before he broke it.

"Commander," the medic said finally, "we sure are glad to have you home."

"Well, thank you," Stafford said. "I sure am glad to be home."

That broke the ice, and the medic went on. "You know, my kids have been praying for you, and they made you something."

He handed Stafford a Welcome Home poster that his children had colored. Stafford thanked the man.

"I was wondering, Commander," the medic said, "if you've got anything I could give them as a souvenir?"

Stafford thought for a moment, and then said, "Sure. How about these clothes?" He began stripping off the jacket, shirt, pants, and shoes that the North Vietnamese had issued for this occasion. By the time the little party had reached the hospital room that was their destination, Stafford was down to his shorts. He slipped into the hospital robe that someone handed him. It felt — and smelled — cleaner than anything he could have imagined.

There were five other POWs in the large room, waiting for whatever came next. A doctor introduced himself and told them that they would be in the hospital for four days of tests and observation. Then they would fly on to the States for comprehensive medical treatment. Another officer, a dentist, said he would examine the men and take care of any immediate problems. When he had finished, he produced a bottle of bourbon.

"This is strictly against regulations, but I thought some of you might like a pull." He poured out a little whiskey in hospital cups.

"Welcome home," the dentist said. Glasses were raised, and they drank.

By now the escort officers had arrived to introduce themselves. The whiskey had been an ad libbed gesture by a sympathetic fellow officer; but everything else about the arrival and treatment of these men had been studied and planned down to the last detail. The Pentagon had spent hundreds of hours working out a program for repatriation in an attempt to cover every contingency and make the process run as smoothly as possible.

A vital element in the plan was the escort officer. One officer was assigned to each returning POW. It was his sole duty to assist the man through the transition, to help him reestablish his life, answer his questions, run his errands, set up his appointments, and generally be available to handle whatever arose. Eventually he would conduct an elaborate debriefing. But that would come later, after the initial shock of reentry had passed. In the first days he would be a buffer and a guide into the mysteries of the real world.

In the early planning there was talk of making one of the POW's old buddies his escort officer. The thinking was that he might appreciate having a friend around, someone who could hold his hand, if necessary, and help him over the rough spots. After more thinking, the officials concluded that this was a bad idea. It would be too hard on both men.

It was finally decided that the escort would be an officer one rank junior to the man he was assigned to assist. This would keep matters militarily correct — the POW could give orders instead of making requests — and would ensure that an escort had enough clout when he spoke on his man's behalf.

Stafford's escort introduced himself as Jack Mahoney, a navy lieutenant commander. He carried a folder full of professional and personal information, as well as a schedule of appointments and the outline of the events that would make up the next few weeks of Stafford's life.

"We have telephones with open lines," he told Stafford, "so you can call home. There is a mess hall available where you can order anything at all that you want to eat. There is a tailor shop with uniforms in your size and tailors standing by to make alterations. We can have a uniform fitted right away, with your current rank and all decorations to which you are entitled. Let me know what you want, and I'll get right on it. For the next few weeks, Commander, just think of me as your personal aide."

Stafford reflected for a minute. Now that he was back, he wanted to be able to think of himself again in the role he had left almost six years earlier, when he had been a working aviator. Now he wanted to dress the part.

"All right," he said. "I want a set of wash khakis with a set of wings and a fore-and-aft cap. I want a wrist watch, a pocket knife, and a wallet with a military ID card and seven hundred dollars in cash."

"Are you sure you don't want dress blues?" the escort asked. "That's what most of the men are wearing."

"I thought you said you were going to be my aide," Stafford said. "Wash khakis and a piss cutter. Can you get them or can't you?"

Mahoney smiled. "Aye, aye, sir."

"Good. Then I want you to tell me how I can get to that mess hall. I want two hot dogs and a Coke."

Before he left, Mahoney took Stafford aside.

Now comes the bad news, Stafford thought. He was ready for it, he thought, whatever it might be; had gone through all the possibilities and prepared himself. There was no need for the chaplain, who was still in the room, waiting to be of assistance and comfort.

But Mahoney had no devastating news to convey. Nobody

in Stafford's immediate family had died. His mother was at home, waiting for a call. Everyone else was fine — older, but fine. Stafford assimilated that news easily enough and waited for the next part. Probably his wife was divorcing him, if she hadn't already. But he had planned for that, too. Certainly he did not need a chaplain to help him digest that news.

"There is one thing," Mahoney said.

"Yes."

"It doesn't usually work this way, but in your case . . . well, your wife is here, in the Philippines. She flew in from Hong Kong, where she is living."

It was the first he'd heard of that. His wife had sent letters, but in the last couple of years they had stopped coming, and Stafford had had no way of knowing whether she had simply stopped writing or the North Vietnamese had not allowed her letters to reach him. Now he knew that, since the last letter, his wife had moved to Hong Kong. And she was here to see him.

"There's a room where you can visit with her as soon as you want."

"Okay. But first I want to take a shower and get into some clean clothes."

"Fine."

It was the first honest shower, with real hot water, that he had taken since that morning before he was shot down. Ever since then, bathing had meant foul, tepid water and harsh lye soap. Here the tiles were clean, and the stainless steel fixtures gleamed. He turned the hot water up until he could barely stand it, poured Phisohex from the plastic container, and soaped himself lavishly. The unimaginably clean smell of the soap did even more than the taste of bourbon whiskey to convince him that he had left the other world behind. He stayed under the water for half an hour or more, using up almost the entire container of Phisohex. Nobody waited for him outside; no guard hurried him.

When he finally got out of the shower and dried off, Stafford looked at himself in the big bathroom mirror. In the camps there had been no mirrors, so you did not know, perhaps mercifully, just how you looked. You could get an idea by examining your reflection in the surface of the dirty water of a cistern or the occasional window pane and you could judge from looking at the other men in the camp, especially those you had known before you were shot down, that you probably looked as bad as they did. But there had been no way to examine yourself fully for the evidence of what captivity had done to you. Now, in the steamy mirror, he did that.

It wasn't so bad. He looked gaunt and he looked older. He'd been in his early thirties when he was shot down; now he was almost forty. Those were years when you started to show your age even under the best circumstances. But he did not look haunted or permanently traumatized. At best he looked like an aging aviator, and at worst he looked as if he had been "rode hard and put up wet," as they used to say in the fleet. The face that looked back at him from the mirror was not cause for either great joy or deep gloom. He looked like what he was — someone who had survived.

The question, of course, was whether or not that face in the mirror was an accurate reflection of the man inside. At this point he did not know, and neither did anyone else. Psychiatrists and other experts had been interviewed for news stories about the POWs when they were first released. Some had predicted that the men would be deeply and enduringly marked by the experience. Some of these experts had been quoted as saying that more than half of these men would require institutionalization; that many of them would suffer from incurable depression; that many could be expected to commit suicide.

Stafford had not felt suicidal since that time in the Green Knobby Room. Now, in the hospital at Clark, after his first real shower and the first good look at himself in years, he felt clean and mildly relieved that he did not look as bad as he had a perfect right to expect. He also felt like getting dressed and meeting his wife. However things would turn out with her, he wanted to get on with it. Those were the first enduring sensations of release — cleanliness and an urge to get on with it, to shift from the passive, fearful, devious gear in which he had been stuck for so long and begin, once again, to take charge, to meet things head on. If she was waiting to tell him she was leaving, then he wanted to get on with that, and then go find that mess hall and eat his two hot dogs and drink his Coke. After that, he would see how they were coming with his uniforms, and then he would call his mother. Next, there were medical and dental appointments, things to talk over with Mahoney . . . all sorts of things that he needed to do. Already he had made out a list in his mind — he'd need a notebook and a pen to keep track — and it felt just goddamned fine to be busy once again.

His wife was waiting for him in a little visiting room. They looked at each other like people who had been set up for a blind date, only instead of checking to see if the other person lived up to previous descriptions, each scanned the other's face for an expression, a vagrant smile or a uncontrollable frown, that would convey how much damage the years apart had caused.

"Hello." It was all Stafford could think to say.

"Hello."

"How are you?"

"I'm fine. How are *you?*"

"Better than I should be. You look great."

"So do you . . ."

"All things considered," he finished.

They embraced, kissed, held each other briefly and tentatively. They had been married for more than six years but had lived together only four months — that was the hard, arithmetical truth about their relationship. Between them was a gulf that measured nearly two thousand days and all that had happened during those days.

They talked for a while, calmly, like travelers between departures. She asked what was next for him. Four days here in the Philippines, he explained, then back to the United States and the hospital at San Diego, where he would be a patient for several weeks at least. He needed dental work and a hernia operation for sure; didn't need a doctor's examination to know that. He might need work on his arm and shoulder; they might have to be rebroken and reset. He didn't know what other medical work might be necessary. He could be in San Diego for months. She could come there and get an apartment . . . "if you still want to be married."

"Well, yes," she said in the same detached tone. "Yes, I do."

He talked about how she could get an apartment and a car and how he would be an outpatient, once the surgery was done, and they could travel and get to know each other again.

"But I live in Hong Kong now," she said.

"Will you be coming to San Diego? I'll be there in four days."

"Yes. But I live in Hong Kong now."

It was a baffling, vague sort of impasse, not the clean, yes-or-no conclusion that Stafford had expected when he asked his wife if she still wanted to be married. As much as anything, what he wanted was an end to uncertainty and ambiguity, wanted hard answers and solutions to the questions that he would face in the next months. Already he was in an area that lacked definition, where the answer, if there was one, was unclear and the facts seemed to be shifting in and out of focus.

They talked a little longer, then Stafford went back to his

room and his wife left to make arrangements to fly to Hong Kong. Before she left, she said she would see him in San Diego.

Stafford made the call to his mother, ate his hot dogs, and then lay down for a while on blessedly clean white sheets. The sensation was like that of bathing with Phisohex — of almost unnerving cleanliness — and it was a while before he could get to sleep. This was a problem for many of the men. Some had trouble sleeping on a mattress and sheets, so they slept on the floor, under a single blanket. Others simply had trouble sleeping anywhere.

For three days Stafford saw doctors and dentists and listened as Mahoney briefed him on what to expect in San Diego and beyond. He was busy and purposeful, and that felt better than he could have imagined. He kept a notebook and a pen in the shirt pocket of his wash khakis, and he made lists and then checked things off once they were done. Dentist for x rays: check. Doctor for hernia exam: check. Internist for worm medicine: check. Talk to Mahoney re pay records: check. With productive days and fresh meals in his belly, Stafford slept well and soundly.

When the group Stafford arrived with had finished at Clark, they boarded the C-141s and took off again, this time for the United States. Stafford felt that he had passed through the initial stages of decompression with no ill effects. The medical examinations had revealed that, yes, he did need surgery to repair two hernias. The dentists said he needed at least one root canal and some bridgework. It was still uncertain whether or not his arm would need to be reset.

He had been brought up to date on his pay records and the decorations and promotion that he had received while he was in captivity. Also, Mahoney had briefed him on what he could expect in the way of future assignments in the navy.

Every effort would be made to get him the job and duty station of his choice, within reason. The navy would help him if he wanted to return to college and finish his degree in order to prepare for a civilian career.

So far, the only inconclusive, ambiguous element in the mix was his relationship with his wife. Other men had come home to worse. Much worse. When they had talked about it, before release, someone had said that when you got home and found yourself facing a lot of problems, you would just have to look at it the same way you would approach eating an elephant — "one leg at a time." Stafford felt as though he had come home to a small elephant. Either his wife would be waiting for him in San Diego, or she wouldn't. Either way he could work it out. Otherwise, he was in control.

So he felt good when he boarded the transport and settled in for the long flight back across the Pacific. Guam, Wake, Midway, Hawaii, and then California. He had spent most of the last ten years on this side of the ocean. Most likely he would never come this way again. He could live with that, he thought.

When the plane was airborne, he struck up a conversation with a nurse and a doctor. In the middle of their conversation, somewhere between Wake and Midway, when it was dark outside and the reading lamps burned dimly inside the airplane, Stafford began to weep. There was no fighting back or swallowing these tears; they came in a flood. He had not cried this way since he was a child, and then he had at least known what was causing him to cry. Here, thirty thousand feet over the Pacific, with a new life, his deliverance, waiting to begin at the end of the flight, he had no idea why he was crying. He had not even realized that he was about to cry. The fit of weeping had come over him with no warning, like lightning out of a cloudless sky. It took almost half an hour for him to stop.

When he did, he apologized to the nurse and doctor. "I don't even know what it was about," he said lamely.

They told him not to worry about it, that they had seen it happen before on earlier flights with men who had been released in the first groups to leave North Vietnam. Actually, they said, it was fairly common. Nothing to worry about.

Stafford tried to put it behind him. No point in feeling embarrassed; he was beyond those small vanities, and besides, it was as though the tears had come, somehow, from outside him, not from within. You don't apologize for a rash or a cold, for something that you catch. Still, he felt uneasy. He knew that the weeping represented a setback in what had so far been a smooth road home. What was worse — since he knew that there would be setbacks even if he could not identify them in advance — was the sense that his feeling of control was more wishful thinking than hard fact; that more and more, things would take him by surprise. He felt, in short, as if he had been blindsided. It would not be the last time.

Seventeen

WHEN STAFFORD ARRIVED in San Diego, his wife was not there to meet him. She came in from Hong Kong a few days later, and they began a futile attempt to stay together, which lasted for almost two years before they were finally divorced.

During those two years some things went better than Stafford would have expected; but from time to time he felt himself once again taken totally by surprise. He suffered from bouts of depression, times when he simply could not do what he knew needed to be done, when the simplest thing suddenly seemed unbearably difficult. There were no violent flashbacks or hallucinations, but there were frequent incapacitating episodes, periods when he felt as helpless as he had when he was locked up alone in the Annex back at Plantation.

He was assigned to the hospital in San Diego for six months. His hernias were repaired and the dental work he needed was done. The doctors decided against rebreaking his arm and prescribed physical therapy instead. He went through a long debriefing, telling his story in detail and looking at hundreds of photographs of men who were missing to establish whether or not he had seen any of them in the camps.

During this time he was sent to Washington for a formal

White House ceremony honoring the POWs. Dinner was
served on the lawn, and John Wayne was on hand to deliver
some remarks. There was dancing, and President Nixon explained what he had done to bring the POWs home and why
it had taken so long.

Stafford also went to Dallas for a ticker-tape parade wel-
coming the POWs and to his hometown, Cambridge, Maryland, for a Memorial Day celebration, where he was honored. These were all heady, if slightly disorienting, occasions,
and Stafford reacted to them with a mixture of genuine
gratitude and the suspicion that he was somehow unworthy
of the attention.

And there was plenty of attention. Hundreds of letters
came in from strangers who had worn bracelets engraved
with his name and the date he was shot down. Those bracelets had been made popular by groups that kept the POW
issue public during the last months of the war, and thousands of people had worn them. The navy provided clerical
help at the hospital so the men could answer the heavy vol-
ume of mail.

There were other unsolicited and touching acts of gener-
osity. Strangers who had time-share condominiums or sail-
boats offered to let POWs use them. The Ford Motor Company leased an automobile to each man for a year and waived
the payments, so Stafford had a Mustang to drive. Western
Airlines offered free air travel. The gifts came without any
strings and without any publicity.

Some offers were not entirely altruistic. Politicians came
to visit, trailing photographers. Stafford and the other POWs
quickly learned that they were there chiefly to borrow a little
glory. The exception was Ronald Reagan, who invited men
up to his ranch but did not allow coverage.

Inevitably people contacted the returning POWs offering
lucrative investment opportunities. Several of these invest-

ments failed, and the men who were involved lost the back pay they had accumulated at such a painful price.

The attention — good and bad — was not always easy to handle, especially when there was so much to relearn and assimilate, and when, like Stafford, a man was wrestling with private difficulties. For a few weeks he and several other men who had come home to problems with their wives lived in a wing of the bachelor officers' quarters at the San Diego base and drew together almost as though they were back in North Vietnam.

Coming home, it turned out, was not as hard as some of the experts had predicted it would be, but it was not easy, either. Stafford and the others were not through bouncing back.

Charlie Plumb, who had been married less than a year when he was shot down and who had fantasized elaborately about the dinners he and his wife would eat, the cities they would travel to, the family they would raise, came home to find that his wife was divorcing him to marry another man. Her lawyers had cited desertion as grounds for the divorce. When he met his wife to talk to her about it, she was already wearing the other man's ring. She returned the one Charlie had given her and said she was very, very sorry.

But, hard as that was, it was survivable. You could bounce back from a divorce.

No matter how the family situation turned out, the POWs still had to move on and decide what to do next. The services tried to make it easy for them, but they had all lost a lot of time, missed assignments on the career ladder, and fallen behind their peers. While they had been promoted according to schedule, they were still, in terms of experience, exactly where they had been on the day they were shot down. It would be next to impossible for them to make up the ground they had lost, especially in the case of young officers like Charlie Plumb, who had been on his first fleet assignment when he was captured and had lost six years on the career path.

Plumb had gone to Annapolis and intended to make the navy his life. He had dreamed of rising from one promotion to the next until he became . . . what? Chief of Naval Operations, maybe. But certainly a flag — the rank of admiral — was not out of the question. That was why they had a naval academy — to train future admirals. He was aggressive and ambitious and he knew where he wanted to go.

But he saw, very clearly, that it was not in the cards. Too much time lost. Reluctantly he left the navy and went into business, helped by friends, family, and sympathetic people who pointed him in the right direction. He made some investments in real estate around his home near Kansas City. The investments were good, and he quickly found himself making more money than he could ever have imagined possible. Ironic, since he had never fantasized about coming home and getting rich.

He also began giving talks based on his experiences in Vietnam. He was good at it and soon found himself in demand by civic groups, business organizations, schools, and churches. He polished his talk and began charging larger and larger fees until, eventually, it became his career. He was represented by the same agent who handled some of the biggest names on the lecture circuit. He also remained active in the Navy Reserve, flying on weekends and going to sea for two weeks in the summer. Finally, he remarried and moved to California, where he built a house, bought a Mercedes, and settled into a life of civilian comfort. It was a kind of bouncing back.

When he was still in Kansas, three years after his release, Plumb got a call one night from Danny Glenn, the man he had shared a cell with at Plantation who used to ask his advice about the house he was planning to build when he got home.

"Charlie, can you come see me? There's something I want to show you."

"Well, all right. Where are you?"

"Oklahoma. Let me tell you how to get here."

Plumb took down the directions and said he would drive down that weekend.

"Great, Charlie. Can't wait to see you."

Plumb followed the directions, and when he made the last of several turns, the one that would take him up to the driveway where he was to turn in, he saw the house. The very same house that he had heard described a thousand times and that he had helped design while his roommate scratched out the plans and prints on the floor of their cell. He stopped the car and studied the house for a long time. It was like something from a dream.

Glenn came out to meet him.

"Hey, Charlie, come on in. Let me show you around."

Everything was there in exact detail. Plumb could walk around the house as though he had lived in it all his life. When he came to the end of a hall and opened a door, he knew exactly what would be on the other side. Knew where every bathroom was and what kind of tile would be on the floor. Nothing was out of place, and nothing had been changed from the way the house was planned, that lifetime ago.

"It's beautiful," he said. "I can't believe you got everything just right."

"Oh, it was a bitch, let me tell you. They'd stopped making a lot of the materials I had in mind when I designed this baby. I had to go to salvage yards and warehouses all across the Southwest to find some of this stuff. But, by God, I wasn't going to compromise. I had too much invested. You know what I mean."

Almost everyone followed up, in one way or another, on some project that had its genesis in Vietnam. The man who had gone into a trance every afternoon in order to play a round of golf in his mind was invited to play in a local tournament, as a kind of celebrity participant, a few weeks after he got home. It was the first time he had held a club since before he was shot down. He played the best round of his life and won the tournament.

When they went out for their first restaurant meal, men who had taken the wine appreciation course ordered a vintage they had learned about in Hanoi. Stafford left the hospital in San Diego to spend a few days in Acapulco, and when he got there he chartered a sailboat using the Spanish he had learned in Dave Luna's class. Jim Shively probably did as well as any man at following through on the promises he had made to himself while he was in captivity. He married a woman who had two children, both girls, and they had two more. So Shively no longer lived his life surrounded by men.

The career decision that had been so tough for Charlie Plumb was something they all had to face. The services offered to send men to civilian schools to compensate them for the time they had lost. Many took them up on it, among them Al Stafford, who finally got his degree. Others, like Shively, resigned and went back to college on their own. He got a law degree and went to work in the office of the U.S. attorney. Ben Ringsdorf went to medical school and opened a clinic near Mobile, Alabama. Hoss Milligan went for a Ph.D. and became the chief veterinarian in the air force.

Some men decided to stay in the service, and some even tried to keep flying. Tom Hall, who had never been a dedicated professional military man, decided that he loved flying and wanted to keep doing it as long as possible. He asked for assignment to a squadron of the new F-14s in the Pacific. Instead, he was given F-4s out of Norfolk.

He went through the Replacement Air Group to learn how to fly the airplane, which he had never liked much. Too big and not agile enough — a very fast tub. In a few months he had completed his retraining, except for the navy pilot's equivalent of final exams: night carrier landings.

When the time came for his test, Hall took off from the naval air station at Oceana, Virginia, and headed out over the Atlantic, where he found the *Forrestal* and got in the pattern. Suddenly, everything that had always seemed so easy and so fluid became difficult and rushed. He felt as though he was *behind* the airplane, fighting it down onto the deck. Sweat seeped into his flight suit, and his throat tightened. He found the meatball, and through sheer force of will put the plane on the deck and caught a wire.

Four to go.

He was launched, got back into the pattern, and came around again. It was no better this time. He felt as though he was physically wrestling with the plane. But he got the wire, again. By the second launch, he was tired.

He brought it around again and got the beast on the deck. And again. Until he had the five requisite landings. The radar operator in the back seat of the F-4, a young man to Hall's thirty, said something about how smoothly he handled the stick.

That kid, Hall thought, *doesn't know how close he came to getting killed.*

He took on some fuel after the last landing, then launched again and pointed it for Oceana. On the short flight home he told himself, *Well, that's it. Time to hang it up.*

He turned in his wings when he got back to the beach and

later resigned his commission. He built houses for a while, then when the real estate market around Norfolk collapsed, he moved down to the coast of North Carolina, on the banks of a small blackwater river, where he built a house and set himself up in the cabinet-making business. He also bought an ultralight airplane — built from aluminum tubing, covered with fabric, and powered by an engine small enough for a lawnmower — a machine that was as far down the spectrum from an F-4 or an F-8 as it was possible to go. Hall assembled the plane from a kit and, with his genius for improvisation, made some alterations to give it better performance. He flew that plane around the swamps and the corn fields near his home, occasionally buzzing a feeding bear. The child who had been born just before he was shot down was in grade school when he got home. He and his wife had three more. They also kept bees and a pet hummingbird that lived in the house, just the way he had described it to his cellmates in Plantation.

Mike Burns, who was twenty-two, unmarried, and had flown only eighteen missions when he was shot down, also wanted to keep flying when he got home. For so much of his life he had been defined as a pilot, so it seemed that he ought to be one for a while. He had not even been flying the plane when he was shot down, had been a mere backseater. So he asked to be requalified and assigned to a squadron.

He qualified but, once more, did not get the assignment he wanted. He began to realize that the military would always be a life of frustration for him, that he did not have the ability of the professional to shrug things off and take what was given him — like those guys in Hoa Lo who could talk about being expendable, as though it were just another set of orders. He resigned his commission.

For a while Burns did nothing. Or, rather, he thought

about what he wanted to do as he traveled, flew around the country, visiting friends and simply staying in motion. Finally, he decided on law school back in Indiana.

When Burns was nearing graduation from law school, he went to Sarasota, Florida, where he was offered a job in a firm, provided he could pass the Florida bar exam. He made arrangements to take the test in Miami and rented a house in Sarasota. He felt himself on the verge, finally, of a new life; ready to put the military and Vietnam behind him.

But there was another bureaucratic foul-up. When he arrived in Miami for the exam, his name was not on the list. Without the proper paperwork he could not take the exam for another six months. He raged and shouted, but nothing changed.

Fortunately the firm in Sarasota was willing to keep him on as a clerk until he could take the exam. After he'd passed and practiced for a couple of years, he went out on his own.

Life in Florida was agreeable. He married and had two children. He bought a home on Sonesta Key, a good address, and kept a sailboat on the canal out back. He'd learned enough about sailing from Al Stafford that it came easy, and on the weekends he would take his family out in the gulf for a few hours. Now and then he and his wife would leave the kids and take an overnight trip somewhere. When he was at home, relaxing, he listened to the music that he had learned to appreciate in those classes held in the dim evening light at Hoa Lo, and he would remember Joe Crecca weeping as he described Mozart's misfortunes.

One night when he was at a party — one of those small, quiet affairs on the lawn of someone's house, with the breeze blowing through the palm trees and the smell of salt water on the air — it came out in conversation that he had been a POW. It was not something he told people, though he didn't go to any trouble to hide it, either. His citations and the decorations he had received for treating the wounds of the men he traveled with to Hanoi and then nursed to health in Hoa Lo were hung on the wall of his office. But he didn't bring it up himself; he had put it behind him.

A woman at the party wanted to talk about his experience, and Burns did his best to satisfy her curiosity.

"How does it make you feel," she asked, "to know that you wasted all those years?"

Burns looked at her for a moment and then said, "Those years weren't wasted. You probably wouldn't understand, but I lived *hard* all that time. Harder than I've ever lived."

He remembered what Shively had said, about how everyone ought to go through it, maybe not for as long as they had, but for a year. That made more sense now than it ever had.

Stafford stayed in the navy. He couldn't fly anymore because of his injuries, so when he returned to active duty he was assigned to a staff position in administration in Washington, moving papers from box A to box B. His wife went with him, although things between them had not gotten better in San Diego, and at one point Stafford had even talked to a lawyer. But when his wife said she wanted to keep trying, he agreed.

He thought that Washington might be good for him, if for no reason than that it was close to home. He could visit his favorite places on the Eastern Shore and, maybe, look for an old farm that he could buy and move to when he retired. He would run the farm the way Hoss Milligan had taught him.

But he learned quickly that the Eastern Shore had changed, and the people who could afford land there were not navy commanders. His problems at home continued, and while the staff job was nothing but routine paperwork, it was also intimidating — so much so that he felt himself over-whelmed from time to time and simply could not function. He experienced what he would later hear described as anxiety attacks. To his way of thinking, he was being blindsided again.

Navy doctors prescribed counseling. There was a psychiatrist at Andrews Air Force Base, where his office was located, but the doctors insisted he drive to Bethesda, where he could see a navy doctor. So twice a week Stafford spent three hours on the Beltway, driving to and from Bethesda Naval Hospital for appointments that were, as often as not, canceled or put off for an hour or two. Meanwhile, he fell farther behind in his work and deeper into a pit of depression. The doctors prescribed drugs, which he took, then wished he hadn't.

He made up his mind to quit seeing the doctors at Bethesda and taking their drugs. If he was ever going to escape the pit, he decided, then he would have to climb out himself. When he told the navy doctor this, he was warned, "We could have you committed."

It was guards and interrogators and threats of punishment all over again.

So Stafford made a plan — almost an escape plan — and in a few weeks, he had arranged a reassignment to Pensacola. It was where he had learned to fly, and he thought of it as a place that had always been good to him. The navy was sending him back to the University of West Florida to finish his degree. He would buy a house and give his marriage another six months.

Going back to school was easy after all the studying he'd done in North Vietnam. The luxury of pencils, paper, books, and a library seemed almost limitless. He did well in class, and the periods of incapacitating panic came less and less frequently. The inevitable divorce was almost painless. He left his wife with the house and moved into small, quiet quarters while he finished school.

He bought a boat, which he named *Spirit*, and lived aboard it at a berth on the Naval Air Station. He took another staff job, and after work he would take the boat out into Pensacola Bay, through the pass, and into the gulf, sometimes staying all night and sailing back in the morning in time to change into his uniform and go to work.

After a few months of living on the boat, he bought a house not far from the base, and then an old step-sider Ford pickup with a flathead six-cylinder engine. He parked the truck behind the house, pulled the engine, took it apart, and began slowly rebuilding it.

Some days he had to force himself to sail or work on the truck. But he knew that those things would make him feel good even when it seemed that they would not. He had told himself, while he was in prison, that these were the things he would do if he ever got home, and now, by God, he was going to do them. Fake it till you make it.

Doing those things *did* make him feel better, helped him bounce back from a lingering depression that had its obvious causes but was no easier to shake for that.

One night in Pensacola Stafford ran into another former POW at a restaurant. He had stayed in close touch with some of the men who had been his supporters in the Big Room — Burns, Hall, Ringsdorf, Shively, and others — but he had never known this man well.

"Hey, Al, baby," the man said, "come on over here. Let me buy you a drink."

Stafford had quit drinking when he got to Pensacola — one of those things that made him feel better — but he joined the man at the bar and ordered a soft drink.

"Ah, come on, have a real drink," the man said. He had plainly had several.

"No, thanks."

The man shrugged and ordered another for himself. They sat at the bar for a while and talked about how things were going. Who had been heard from and what had happened to old so-and-so, who had been promoted and who had gotten out and gone on to other things.

Eventually the other man turned solemn and pensive and looked deep into his glass.

"You know, Al, I used to tell myself, when we were over there, that if I ever got home, I wasn't going to say one word about it. I wasn't going to talk about it, think about it, read about it, watch anything on television about it. It was going to be like the blue sky behind you — wasted air space. But you know what?"

"What's that?" Stafford asked indulgently.

"I am a sonofabitch if sometimes I don't miss it."

Stafford never missed it. Never came even close to missing it. But it did seem as though he had lived with it more or less constantly ever since he'd been back. Something was changing, though. In a way he was making the experience work to his advantage. He thought less and less about what it had done *to* him and more about what it had done *for* him.

After a year of staff work, Stafford took command of the survival school at Pensacola. He was responsible for teaching young aviators what he knew about survival, and he felt that he could teach them a lot. He kept the job for four years before retiring in 1979, and he considered it the most successful tour of his career. His seniors agreed and gave him outstanding fitness reports.

In addition to finding a way to translate the experience of North Vietnam into some kind of useful work, Stafford found himself reliving moments from that experience in the most unexpected ways. When he dismantled the truck engine and began putting it back together, he saw the faces of Joe Crecca and Tom Hall. The valve guides were just where they'd said they would be, and when he sheared a bolt, he was able to torque it free the way they had taught him. When he was crossing Lake Okeechobee and the diesel in his sailboat quit, he took the injectors off to clean them, and, remembering with absolute clarity the lecture he had sat through at Hoa Lo, was careful to remove the crush washer so it did not fall into the cylinder. There were so many lessons that he had learned, large and small. Once again, they were helping him to bounce back.

Eighteen

IMMEDIATELY AFTER THE POWs returned from Vietnam, a navy flight surgeon, Captain Robert Mitchell, organized a study. Every man was given a complete physical as well as a battery of tests and several interviews with a psychologist. He was to return and retake all these tests every year, for as long as Mitchell could keep the program alive. Every man was assigned a counterpart who was as close as possible to him in age, physical characteristics, and experience but had not been a POW. The men in this control group were to be given the same annual examinations and tests. The data, it was hoped, would yield useful conclusions about the long-term effects of this kind of captivity.

Fifteen years after the program was started, Mitchell had discovered some interesting, even startling facts. First, the men who returned were in surprisingly good health, all things considered. They suffered the lingering effects of untreated injuries, but otherwise their general health was better than that of the men in the control group, especially in terms of their cardiovascular condition, which could be accounted for by the fact that POWs seldom ate any red meat or other fatty foods. More men in the control group suffered heart attacks than did the returning POWs.

More remarkably, the POWs generally showed an increase in their IQ scores. The classes they had held and the games of concentration that they had played had paid off beyond keeping them diverted while they were in their empty cells. Furthermore, the POWs did not seem to suffer from any lingering emotional problems that could be traced to their captivity. They experienced the same frustrations and anxieties as the men in the control group, and in fact showed a slightly greater ability to deal with stress — something else they had learned in Hanoi.

There were no long-term psychiatric problems. None of the POWs had been committed. There was only one suicide. A few, like Stafford, had suffered bouts of depression, but the numbers were not out of line with the average. While one man had probably lost a chance at high flag rank because of depression, several other POWs did go on to senior positions in the navy and air force. Two had been elected to the U.S. Senate, including John McCain, who had risked punishment to get a message of support to Al Stafford in solitary. (The other was Jeremiah Denton, who had blinked out the word *torture*.) The experience, grim as it had been, had not ruined these men or made them fit only for some kind of meager, marginal life once they were back home. They had truly bounced back.

Mitchell, who is still studying the data, became something of a father figure to the POWs who took part in his program. He takes a nonscientific pride in the way they have turned all the dire predictions upside-down. He believes that their spirit of teamwork and resistance, their ingenuity, is behind this remarkable outcome. "They were well-trained, well-motivated men who believed in something," he said. "A similar group, taken at random, probably wouldn't have done nearly so well."

The services incorporated the lessons of Bounce Back into their doctrine and now teach it at their survival schools, where some of the POWs, including Douglas Hegdahl, lecture on their experiences in Vietnam.

The POWs themselves have assimilated. What might have been seen as a shameful episode is an experience they do not hide or shrink from. They have moved on, most of them, and put it behind them, but they do still keep in touch. A newsletter, the *Free Press*, is published irregularly and sent out to all the names on a constantly updated mailing list. It contains news of recent retirements, moves, sometimes deaths. When Nick Rowe — who had been a prisoner in South Vietnam for five years, escaped, and went home to publicize the POW issue — was killed by guerrillas in the Philippines in April 1989, the paper carried an obituary that ended with the words: "Nam-POWs send our sincerest condolences to Nick's family and his many close friends over the loss of this very special man — the toughest of the tough." It concluded with the tap code sign-off, "GBU & CUL, Nick."

Every two years a reunion is held somewhere, and former POWs come from all over the country to socialize and remember for a couple of days. Al Stafford drove to Washington in June 1989 for one of these reunions. He had been retired from the navy for ten years. Things had turned out well for him. He had married again. He and his wife had just spent four months sailing on his new boat, *Fiddler's Green*, in the Bahamas. He had come home to Pensacola just for this reunion.

Stafford found some of the old guys at the hotel where the gathering was held. Mike Burns was there, carrying his infant daughter; Charlie Plumb; Guy Gruters, who had taught the math courses. They visited like alums returning to the university for homecoming after twenty years.

The reunion was a combined affair. It included both the Fourth Allied POW Wing and the Red River Rats, men who had flown missions over North Vietnam but had not necessarily been shot down. The two groups mingled, but, more often than not, the former POWs spent most of their time with those they had shared space with at the prison camps, even though they rarely talked about those days. Conversation turned, instead, on the domestic, prosaic elements of life now: new babies, new jobs, new wives.

During a cocktail party on the first evening of the reunion, Stafford was standing off a little from the crowd, looking for a familiar face, when someone shouted his name, ran across the room, and leaped into his arms. For a moment, holding the man up and trying to keep his balance, Stafford did not know who this guy was. "Al, baby," the man shouted. "God, it's great to see you, man. I've been worrying about you for twenty years."

It turned out to be John Roosen, the man whose place Stafford had taken in the alpha strike on the day he was shot down.

"Great to see you, too, John," Stafford said. "You mind if I put you down?"

Then Roosen turned serious. "Al, listen, you understand, don't you? I mean, there was no way I could fly that bird that day. It was just *pouring* hydraulic fluid."

"For Christ's sake, John."

"No, I'm serious. Tell me you understand. It's been on my mind for twenty years."

"I understand. What do you think I am?"

"Al, man, I think you are the greatest."

Stafford did not give himself that much credit. In the more than fifteen years he had been home, he had thought about it a lot. He was no hero, that was for sure, and it had always made him uncomfortable when people seemed to think he was. He had been touched, like all of the POWs, by the gestures of sympathy and the offers of kindness since he came home. But he did not think he was a hero.

For a long time he had thought that he might be something considerably less; that he could have been tougher, resisted more, done a better job leading the Big Room. Plenty of men had taken more and bounced back sooner. These thoughts had contributed to Stafford's long-running depression, and he knew it. But he had come to terms with that, too. He had decided that he was an average member of a very special group. If you ranked resisters on a scale from one to ten, he was probably a five or six, and at last he could live with that.

It had been a terrible experience, he would tell friends when he talked about it. Terrible. He couldn't even agree with Shively that it was something that everyone ought to experience for just a year. But like Burns, he would not allow himself to think of those years as wasted. He had made the best of them — the absolute best that anyone could make of them — and there was some pride and solace in that. In some ways he was a better man for having survived, though that did not mean he was glad that he'd gone through all he had or, given the chance, that he would do it again. Not in a million years.

But it was behind him now, behind all of them. He had plans for the rest of his life. After this reunion he would meet his wife back in Pensacola, and then, later in the summer, they would drive out West, to a part of the country he had never seen. He was going to visit the town of Fairplay, Colorado, which, he'd discovered, did indeed exist. Though it was hard to imagine living away from the water and his boat, he thought he might like to own a little spread out there, run a few head of cattle, cut his own wood for the winter, and fish the streams for trout, the way Arv Chauncey had taught him back in Warehouse One. It was one of the few things he had told himself he would do when he got home that he still had not done.

And if anyone in Fairplay wanted to talk to him about his years as a prisoner in Vietnam, he would tell them what he told everyone these days. He would smile and say politely, "I'm sorry, but I only remember the funny parts."